Amos
Doing What Is Right
A Study Guide

Amos
Doing What Is Right
A Study Guide

Robert G. Baker

Smyth & Helwys Publishing, Inc.®
Macon, Georgia

ISBN 1-57312-020-0

Amos: Doing What Is Right. A Study Guide
Robert G. Baker

Copyright © 1995
Smyth & Helwys Publishing, Inc.
6316 Peake Road
Macon, Georgia 31210-3960
1-800-747-3016

Library of Congress Cataloging-in-Publication

Baker, Robert G.
    Amos: doing what is right. A study guide/
    Robert G. Baker
    viii + 136 pp.   5.5 x. 8.5 (14 x 21.5 cm.)
    Includes bibliographical references.
    ISBN 1-57312-020-0
    1. Bible. O. T. Amos—Study and teaching. I. Title.
    BS1585.5.B35 1995
    224'.8'007—dc20   95-4896
                                                 CIP

Contents

In Memory of my Father
Salin Baker, Jr.
1926–1994

Preface

I was first introduced to a study of the book of Amos during my sophomore year at Georgetown College in an Old Testament introduction class taught by Joe Lewis. A gifted scholar and teacher, Dr. Lewis made Amos—both the man and the message—come alive. A few years later, my appreciation for Amos was further enhanced at Southern Seminary in Louisville, Kentucky through the insightful teaching of Dr. Roy Honeycutt. Both of these men have taught me—through their lifestyles as well as through their lectures—what it means to practice justice and righteousness. How blessed I have been because of their influence and example.

The writing of this book would not have occurred without the encouragement and commitment of many people. I am grateful to Smyth & Helwys and especially to Scott Nash for the opportunity to write this study guide. Special thanks go to my friend and secretary, Jackie Clark, for typing this manuscript, and to Hank Ellington, minister of education and administration at Calvary Baptist Church where I am privileged to serve as pastor, for his willingness to edit this work. Above all, I want to thank my wife, Deborah, and my three children, Katy, Nan, and John Robert, for their understanding and support while I worked on this project. They have done more than their share of "holding down the fort at home" so that I could have time at my office for writing and research.

Amos' key concepts of justice and righteousness were modeled to me by my parents, Salin and Syble Baker. They taught me the value of having right relationships with God, others, and myself. They instilled in me early on the principle of justice—knowing and doing what is right. On

Thanksgiving Day last November, my father lost a battle with cancer and died. But the spirit of his legacy—a legacy of justice and righteousness—lives on. This book is dedicated to his memory.

Using This Book

Finally a word to the reader. This book has been written with the assumption that you will have an open text of Amos before you as you read and study. I have used the New Revised Standard Version (NRSV) as the basis for my commentary. With an open Bible and an open mind, join me as we study Amos. Not only in your reading and study but in each area of your life, may you "let justice roll down like waters, and righteousness like an ever-flowing stream" (Amos 5:24).

Robert G. Baker
Spring, 1995
Lexington, Kentucky

Introduction

> "No prophet delivered his oracles to a vacuum.
> . . . History and the prophetic insight were
> matched, as together they provided the media
> for a divine revelation."
>
> –Eric Rust
> *Covenant and Hope*

What do you think about when you hear the word "prophet"? What images are conjured up in your mind whenever that word is used? A crystal ball gazer? A future events predictor? An Ouija board user? A seance convener? An "end of the world" prognosticator?

The Hebrew word for prophet is *nabi'* a word that refers to one who has been chosen to deliver and proclaim a message on behalf of another. The "another" for whom Old Testament prophets spoke and delivered a specific message was God! In fact, these prophets often prefaced their messages and remarks with the formula "Thus says the Lord" (for example, Amos 1:3, 9, 13).

The Lord's words to a particular people via the prophets focused more on the present than on the past or the future. Granted, at times prophets reminded people of the history of their faith, particularly calling them to remember how God had provided deliverance and guidance (3:1-2). Prophets also referred to future happenings, especially in terms of how such happenings would be the result of choices and decisions that people made in the present. Yet, the prophets were largely concerned with the present: delineating wrong conduct; calling for repentance; and reminding folks of God's judgment, forgiveness, and grace (2:6-8; 5:14-15; 6:1-8).

Old Testament prophets, then, were actually preachers and/or proclaimers more than they were predictors. Their primary task was to proclaim a message from God to a particular people in a particular historical setting.

Amos is often regarded as the first of Israel's writing prophets. Although there were certainly other prophets prior to Amos (Elijah, Elisha, and Nathan), Amos was the first prophet to have had a book named after him. Along with Hosea, Isaiah, and Micah, we regard Amos as one of the leading prophets of the eighth century B.C., known as the "golden age" of Israelite prophecy.

The general historical setting of the book of Amos is identified in the book's opening verse:

> The words of Amos, who was among the shepherds of Tekoa, which he saw concerning Israel in the days of King Uzziah of Judah and in the days of King Jeroboam son of Joash of Israel, two years before the earthquake.

Here, at the outset of the book, we are told that Amos lived and ministered during the reigns of two fairly well-known biblical kings: Uzziah, ruler of Judah from 783–742 B.C., and Jeroboam II, the king of Israel from 786–746 B.C.

Throughout our study, keep in mind that the "holy land" of Amos' day was not a united nation. Upon the death of King Solomon in 922 B.C., the united kingdom of Israel split into two separate countries: the northern kingdom, known as Israel with Samaria as its capital city, and the southern kingdom, known as Judah with its capital city Jerusalem. For just over 200 years (922–721 B.C.) Israel and Judah existed side by side as two separate, and to some extent rival, nations.

The following list of Israel's kings might be helpful as we attempt to keep the ministry of Amos in its proper historical context:

The United Monarchy

Saul	1020–1000 B.C.
David	1000–961 B.C.
Solomon	961–922 B.C.

The Divided Monarchy

Judah	**Israel**
Rehoboam (922–915)	Jeroboam I (922–901)
Abijam (915–913)	
Asa (913–873)	
	Nadab (901)
	Baasha (900–877)
	Elah (877–876)
	Zimri (876)
	Omri (876–869)
Jehoshaphat (873–849)	
	Ahab (869–850)
	Ahaziah (850-849)
Jehoram (849–842)	Jehoram (849–842)
Ahaziah (842)	Jehu (842–815)
Athaliah (842–837)	
Jehoash (837–800)	
	Jehoahaz (815–801)
	Jehoash (801–786)
Amaziah (800-783)	
	Jereboam II (786–746)
Uzziah (783–742)	
	The Fall of Samaria (722–721)

By the time that Uzziah and Jeroboam II were reigning respectively in Judah and Israel, more than 165 years had passed since the split of the old united monarchy in 922 B.C. For the most part, Judah was overshadowed by Israel. Israel's geographical location at the crossroads between Egypt and Mesopotamia enhanced its political and economic development. Judah, however, was more isolated in the hill country that was off the major trade routes. In addition, most of the major prophets up to this point in history such as Elijah, Elisha, and Micah (and Hosea just a few years after Amos) were located in the northern kingdom. Both politically and prophetically, at this juncture in history Judah was regarded as the weaker nation.

Why all of this "pre-book-of-Amos" history? Amos did not prophesy in a vacuum. The fact that he ministered during what we now call the period of the divided monarchy certainly had a tremendous impact upon both his work and his reception as a prophet. As verse 1 declares, Amos was from Tekoa, a village about eleven miles south of Jerusalem in the southern kingdom of Judah. Yet, notice that Amos' ministry took place in the northern kingdom of Israel. In essence, Amos was a Confederate citizen called to preach to a Union audience on Yankee turf!

So you can imagine something of the reception that Amos received in Israel when people found out he was from down South. "What could a southerner possibly teach us about God and religion?" the Israelites of Jeroboam II's day must have reasoned. When Amos' message turned out to be rather critical of the northern lifestyle and religion, he was basically told to shut up and go home. We might say that Amos was a southerner called to prophesy to his sometimes "smug-and-uppity-we're-better-than-you-are" brothers and sisters in the North!

In addition to informing us that Amos' ministry in Israel occurred during the reigns of Uzziah in the South and Jeroboam II in the North, verse 1 yields another bit of information relating to the dating of Amos: "two years before the earthquake." Also mentioned in Zechariah 14:5, this earthquake is dated by archaeologists as occurring around 760 B.C. Assuming that this date is fairly accurate, we can project a date for Amos' ministry in Israel somewhere in the vicinity of 760 B.C.

The content of Amos' message also aids us in identifying when the prophet's ministry took place. A close reading of the book of Amos seems to reflect a time during the height of Jeroboam II's reign. For instance, in Amos 6:13-14 the prophet looks back upon some of the previous military victories of Jeroboam II that allowed the borders of Israel to be expanded (2 Kgs 14:25). Such "looking back" on the past achievements of Jeroboam II suggests that Amos' ministry occurred several years after the beginning of Jeroboam II's reign (786 B.C.) when sufficient time had passed for the king's administration to have been firmly established.

Based upon the historical conditions reflected in the content of Amos' preaching as well as the historical information contained in Amos 1:1, most scholars assign a date ranging from 760–750 B.C. to Amos' ministry. For our purposes in this study, a date of around 760 B.C. will be used.

What else should we know (what else can we know) about this southern prophet who ventured North to prophesy to his Yankee cousins around 760 B.C. when King Jeroboam and his Israelite subjects were apparently doing quite well? For some answers, we turn to an overview of the times, the man, the structure of the book, and the message.

The Times

"It was the best of times; it was the worst of times."
Charles Dickens originally penned these familiar words in
regard to Paris in the eighteenth century A.D. If the perceptive Dickens had lived and written in the eighth century
B.C. Israel of Amos' day, his now famous quotation would
have been just as appropriate and accurate. From a political, economic, social, and religious perspective, times in 760
B.C. Israel were good—extremely good! Yet, paradoxically,
the times from each of these perspectives could be perceived as bad—extremely bad.

Consider the *political situation*. Under Jeroboam II's
leadership, Israel enjoyed some of the best years of pros-
perity and peace in its history. A summary of Jeroboam II's
reign can be found in 2 Kings 14:23-29. A close reading of
these verses indicates that Jeroboam II was able to expand
Israel's borders so that they were equivalent to the national
boundaries that had existed during the "glory years" of
King Solomon (2 Kgs 14:25; 1 Kgs 8:65). Even the biblical
historian who was not especially fond of Jeroboam II (2
Kgs 14:24) had to concede that God accomplished some positive things on behalf of Israel by the hand of this king (2
Kgs 14:27). Politically, the times were good.

Yet, for the especially astute observer of international politics (which Amos was), the times were politically
favorable, not so much due to Israel's political prowess as
the result of other factors: the weakness of Egypt to the
Southwest, Syria to the North, and Assyria to the Northeast. Throughout biblical history, the only times that Israel
and/or Judah achieved a modicum of political strength on

a world scale were those occasions when the major players such as Egypt, Syria, Assyria (and later Babylon) were either weak, distracted, or too busy with more pressing issues to be concerned with tiny Israel/Judah. So for persons with eyes to see—both retroactively to past occurrences and in anticipation of future days when one of these major players would regain power and strength—the political times were not totally good.

Ahead of his time, Amos realized the false sense of political security that existed in the land. (In this regard, his preaching was a foretelling). So he sounded a warning that, as we shall see, was largely ignored. Without mentioning Assyria, Amos knew that the menace of Assyria (or some other international power) was looming on the horizon, but "politically secure" Israel was too complacent to hear. As a result, the political times, though good, were paradoxically bad! The threat of the "as-of-yet-unidentified" Assyria lingered. Consequently, the political times while good were simultaneously and paradoxically bad!

This "best-of-times-worst-of-times" paradox also characterized the *economic situation*. As Israel made the transition from a rural to a more commercial lifestyle, a wealthy upper class began to emerge. These "nouveau rich" became quite rich quite rapidly. The content of Amos' preaching indicates just how rich they were: rich enough to have expensive homes that were elaborately decorated and furnished (5:11, 6:4), rich enough to have both winter and summer houses (3:15), rich enough to enjoy fine dining featuring prime cuts of meat and expensive wine leisurely consumed while listening to the pleasant and soothing strains of contemporary music (6:4-6). Such an opulent lifestyle supported by profitable, booming businesses (8:5) demonstrates that economically it was the best of times.

Yet, for many people in Israel, the reign of Jeroboam
II resulted in rapidly declining economic conditions. As the
rich got richer, the poor became poorer. Rather than using
their ever increasing fortunes to assist those who were less
fortunate, the "new rich" of Amos' day actually mistreated
the poor through numerous unscrupulous measures such
as overcharging in the marketplace (8:5), selling poor quality products (8:6), buying and selling the poor as slaves
(2:6), and bribing judges to assure that the poor would seldom if ever receive justice through the court system (8:12).

In short, the financial fortunes of many wealthy
Israelites were obtained by systematically mistreating,
cheating, enslaving, and oppressing the poor. Even as more
and more Israelites joined the ranks of the rich and famous,
more and more Israelites found themselves slipping below
the poverty line. From an economic perspective, it was
simultaneously the best and worst of times.

The ever widening gap between rich and poor contributed to another "best-of-times-worst-of-times" scenario:
namely, what was happening to Israel's *social structure*. Originally, Israel had been a covenant community in which
there were minimal social class distinctions. Indeed, this
covenant community began with all Israelites sharing the
same bottom-rung position on the social ladder—namely,
as slaves in Egypt! Even after God delivered them from
Egyptian slavery via the Exodus experience, the once "bot-
tom-of-the-rung" Hebrew slaves remained on equal footing
as far as social status was concerned. Although they did
not have much in terms of possessions or power, the Israelites did have each other.

As members of a covenant community, all Israelite
males were regarded as equals before God, the law, and
each other. Mutual caring and concern for each other

characterized covenant community life even during the first several centuries of Israel's life together in the Promised Land. During the eighth century B.C., however, the emergence of wealthy and poor social classes contributed to the rapid decline of the mutual family-like concern that had previously characterized Israel.

Instead of using their wealth to enhance the lives of all Israelites, the wealthy members of the community focused almost exclusively on enhancing their own status, power, and financial portfolios! Not only were the needs of poorer Israelites ignored, but the plight of these less fortunate "family members" actually worsened as the wealthy class went so far as to cheat, abuse, and even enslave poorer members of the covenant community in order to enhance their own social and financial status.

In short, mutuality was out; selfishness and "me-ism" were in. The meaning of covenant community was forgotten! Though better for some people, the social times were worse for others. From a social perspective, the Dickens dichotomy of being the best and yet the worst of times held true.

The "best of times worst of times" paradox was also indicative of *Israel's religion.* From an external, statistical perspective, the people of Israel were extremely religious. Attendance at temple services was high (4:4; 5:21)—Sunday School campaigns and high attendance Sabbaths were not needed! Tithes and offerings were given generously and regularly (4:4-5)—budget deficits were unheard of, and annual stewardship drives or periodic capital campaigns were unnecessary!

Worship experiences replete with melodious instrumental and vocal music were well-planned and performed with an air of professionalism (5:21-23)—ill prepared, unplanned, "off-the-cuff-whatever-happens-happens" worship services were certainly not the order of the day! The annual reports and associational letters of the Israelite churches were glowingly impressive. These were certainly not irreligious folks to whom Amos prophesied and preached. Religious activity was at or near a record setting pace.

Yet, all was not well in the religious realm. Though well-attended, well-planned, and externally impressive, religious services and activities were actually quite superficial and shallow. The religion of the Israelites had degenerated into an outward show devoid of internal reality. Such "go-through-the-motions" worship activities had even duped some Israelites into believing that being God's chosen people entailed special privilege without special responsibility. Consequently, "Sunday (actually Sabbath) worship" had no apparent relationship to how one related to one's neighbors (especially the poor) once "church" was over.

External religion was at an all-time high. Heart-felt religion was near a record low. What a paradoxical situation characterized eighth-century B.C. Israel during King Jeroboam II's reign! Not only politically, economically, and socially, but even religiously, it was the best and the worst of times. Into such paradoxical times God sent Amos to prophesy. Just who was Amos, this so-called first of the writing prophets for whom an Old Testament book is named?

The Man

Biographical information about Amos is sparse. Aside from the book that bears his name, Amos is mentioned nowhere else in any other biblical book. Even the book of Amos yields precious little information regarding Amos the man. Our scant information must be gleaned from the book's opening verse (1:1); the narrative describing the prophet's encounter/confrontation with Amaziah, the priest of Bethel (7:10-17); and the descriptions of Amos' visions (7:1-9; 8:1-3; 9:1-4). Such "gleanings," however, provide us with enough information to ascertain something of the essence of this eighth-century B.C. prophet.

His Town

We have already noted that Amos was from Tekoa, a small village south of Jerusalem near the Dead Sea in Judah. Now Tekoa was not exactly the leading commercial center and/or top-rated tourist attraction in the southern kingdom. It certainly was not the type of place where you would want to go for spring break, summer vacation, or even on a religious pilgrimage. Barren and desolate, Tekoa was surrounded on three sides by limestone cliffs. The fourth side, which opened to the East, was not much better: it faced the Dead Sea! George Adam Smith provided what is now regarded as a classic description of Tekoa: "It gave the ancient natives of Judea, as it gives the mere visitor of today, the sense of living next door to doom."[1]

"Where are you from?" is a question we curious humans often ask when we are introduced to someone we don't know. Amos' answer to such a question needs to be kept in mind as we attempt to know him better through our study of the book that bears his name. For as long as we associate Amos with Tekoa, we will remember that he was a citizen of Judah who ministered for God in the rival northern nation of Israel. As long as we recall that Amos was from "living-next-door-to-doom" Tekoa, we will be more prone to acknowledge a critical insight about God—namely, that your origin is not so important to the Lord as is who you are and especially who you have the potential to become.

His Name

Another introductory type question we often ask is "What is your name?" Probably the name Amos is derived from a Hebrew verb meaning "to load" or "to carry a load." Amos' name, then, means something like "burden-bearer" or "burdened." Hebrew names were often thought to reflect something of the character or essence of the person so named. In this regard, Amos' name suited him well. Being from the South yet called to minister in the North was burden enough, but being called to proclaim a message of God's judgment against one's northern Israelite neighbors? A very burdened burden-bearer Amos was! The ministry load he was asked to carry was a heavy one indeed!

His Vocation

In addition to "Where are you from?" and "What is your name?" another question of introduction we usually pose is "What do you do?" or "What is your job?" Amos was a shepherd, but not just any shepherd! We must not automatically assume that he was a common shepherd who scratched out a living by leading a few sheep from pasture to pasture. The Hebrew word translated shepherd in Amos 1:1 is *noqed*. This is not the more common word for shepherd (*ro'eh*). *Noqed* occurs again only in 2 Kings where it is translated "sheep breeder" in reference to King Mesha of

Moab who dealt with thousands of sheep. A *noqed* probably referred to one who owned sheep and who had other shepherds working for him. As a *noqed*, then, Amos could very well have been a respected and successful person in his community.

Amos 7:14 provides additional vocational information. Here, Amos describes himself as a herdsman and a "dresser of sycamore trees." "Dressing" a sycamore tree evidently involved pinching or piercing the tree's figlike fruit so that it would ripen and become edible. The reference to sycamore trees is intriguing since sycamores do not grow in the region of Tekoa with its high altitude and cool climate. Active involvement in the sycamore trade would have called for seasonal travel to a more semi-tropical climate such as could be found in the Jordan valley. Amos did more, then, than keep a few sheep. He was a rather large-scale shepherd-farmer in his day.

Although he was called to prophesy, Amos was quick to remind anyone that he was not a professional prophet (7:14). He regarded himself as a layman. He had not been to seminary, he was not licensed to preach, he had not been "ordained," and he did not serve as a paid member of a church staff.

We will deal more with Amos' vocation when we explore his encounter with Amaziah, the priest of Bethel, who possessed "paid clergy status" (Amos 7:10-17). For now, suffice it to say that—from a vocational perspective—Amos was a respected and perceptive "shepherd-farmer" from the South who dared to respond "yes" when he experienced God calling him to journey North and preach to Israel.

His Call

We are not given many specifics regarding the call experience of Amos. Yet, what information we do have is quite significant. Through his disclaimer (7:14) that he was "no prophet or a prophet's son," Amos declared that "being a prophet" was not his means of earning a living. He was evidently not remunerated for his preaching ministry in Israel.

Based on the reception he received, it is all but certain that he would not have had any contributors if a love offering had been taken or if an honorarium or per diem expenses had been requested. He would not have been eligible to participate in whatever annuity program the full-time professional prophets of his day had! Amos' call, then, was to interrupt his shepherding/farming career so that he could take a mission trip up North! After completing his prophesying assignments—that is, after being run out of the country—Amos in all likelihood journeyed back to Judah to resume his career.

Amos was called to service and ministry as a lay-person, not as a "professional" preacher/prophet. Indeed, there are strong indications (1:1; 7:14-15) that Amos received his call while working at his secular job. We are told in Amos 1:1 that he was "among the shepherds of Tekoa" when he "saw" the light concerning his call to do mission for God. Amos 7:15 suggests that Amos was at work as a shepherd when the Lord called him: "The Lord took me from following the flock, and the Lord said to me 'Go, prophesy to my people Israel.' "

And go Amos did. It was as if he had to go. He perceived God's call so strongly that he felt compelled to respond. His call was no "still small voice" or "go-if-you-feel-like-it" experience. It must have been more like a "Damascus road" phenomenon. Amos likened it to the roaring of a lion (1:2).

On several other occasions, Amos refers to lions (3:4, 8, 12; 5:19). As a shepherd, Amos was highly cognizant of the immediate terror that a lion's roar could cause for sheep and shepherd alike. The roar of a lion— signaling crisis, terror, judgment—demanded an immediate response. God's call to Amos while he was shepherding sheep was comparable to the roaring of a lion. It demanded an immediate response. This was no "let-me-think-about-things-for-awhile-get-my-sheep-rounded-up-and-I'll-get-back-to-you-later" situation. Rather this was God calling. The Lion (of heaven) had roared! Amos had received a call from the Lord; he had to respond!

Amos evidently recognized God's call through a series of visions he experienced (or "saw" in accordance with 1:1). The specifics of the five visions that are recorded in the book of Amos (7:1-3, 4-6, 7-9; 8:1-3; 9:14) will be dealt with later. Note at this juncture, however, that these visions represent very powerful and personal encounters with God through which Amos recognized the Lord calling him to journey to Israel and preach.

For the perceptive, visionary, shepherd-farmer Amos, the result of these visionary experiences was clear. God had called. The Lion had roared. Amos had received a word from the Lord, and he had to share it. What was this word or message that Amos felt so compelled to proclaim? We now turn to an overview of the message of Amos.

The Message

Amos was a doomsday prophet. His primary message was to announce the imminent destruction of Israel! Small wonder, then, that his preaching was unpopular and that the duration of his ministry was relatively brief. Israelites did not want to hear "hell-fire-and-brimstone-your-time-is-almost-up" sermons, especially from a southerner. Yet, all of Amos' prophetic pronouncements were predicated upon his belief that Israel's days were numbered.

As historically documented, Amos' "the-end-is-near" message was absolutely accurate. Although never specifically mentioning Assyria as the instrument of God's judgment against the northern kingdom, Amos was politically perceptive enough to notice the Assyrian threat on the horizon. So following Amos' ministry when Israel fell to Assyria in 722 B.C., the accuracy of Amos' indictingly candid preaching was confirmed. God's judgment had fallen upon Israel.

Why such harsh divine judgment? Why such a negative-oriented message of doom and gloom? Amos 3:10 provides the answer: "They [Israel] do not know how to do right, says the Lord." Yet, "doing right" should have been well-known by Israel. Indeed, God had entered into a covenant relationship with the nation (3:2), but Israel believed the covenant with God meant privilege. The nation forgot that responsibility to live by God's laws—to "do what was right"—was also part of the covenant package.

From the perspective of Amos, the most critical manifestation of Israel "not doing what was right" was in its oppression of the "poor," also referred to as the "needy," the "weak," the "afflicted" and the "righteous." The more well-to-do Israelites were "walking all over" these "little people" in all sorts of ways including buying and selling them as slaves (2:6; 8:6), cheating them in the marketplace through overpricing and shortchanging (8:4-5), violating their legal rights through bribery and other unethical judicial practices (5:10, 12-15), and—although they were also part of the covenant community—ignoring them (6:6).

Injustice toward and oppression of the less fortunate were not the only areas where Israel "did not do right." Growing affluence among the new upper class had resulted in opulent lifestyles characterized by selfishness and greed, often at the expense of the poor and less fortunate (4:1; 5:11; 6:1-6; 8:4-6). As we have already noted, the vibrant, well-attended religious services were void of any real internal meaning. Soaring church attendance had little or no positive impact on how the Israelites treated each other or conducted themselves when church was not in session (4:4-5; 5:21-23).

In the oppression of the poor, the unethical judicial system, the selfish "me-ism" of affluent lifestyles, and the superficial institutional religion that was void of inner meaning Israel did not do (and perhaps in a sense no longer knew how to do) what was right. Such un-right (unrighteous) action put Israel in the precarious position of being diametrically opposed to what God required of covenant people. Precisely what did the Lord require and expect? Amos 5:24, which is arguably the key verse in the entire book, provides the answer. Speaking via the prophet Amos, God declared: "But let justice roll down like waters and righteousness like an ever-flowing stream."

Yet, there was scarcely a trickle of justice or a drip of righteousness in eighth-century B.C. Israel. Right conduct was not in vogue. The promotion of self at the expense of oppressing others was the order of the day. God was displeased. The Lord's patience had been stretched to the breaking point. Judgment was at hand. The Lion (of heaven) had indeed roared. The impact of such divine roaring would be divine punishment described in the imagery that the people of Amos' world would understand: "The pastures of the shepherds wither, and the top of Carmel dries up" (1:2).

Amos, the burden bearer, was called by God to carry this heavy-laden message of doom to his northern cousins. Such judgment had not come without warning. Through occurrences in nature and happenings in history (4:6-12), Israel had been alerted to impending judgment if it did not repent, but such warnings went unheeded. God's judgment, portrayed as Israel's overthrow by an enemy army (3:11-15; 5:3, 5; 6:8-12), was at hand. So certain was God's judgment that Amos actually sang a funeral dirge for Israel:

> Fallen no more to rise
> is maiden Israel;
> forsaken on her land,
> with no one to raise her up. (5:2)

"Fallen no more to rise" sounds rather final, doesn't it? This strong "doom and gloom" proclamation is echoed in other passages that declare Samaria/Israel "shall fall and never rise again" (5:18-20; 8:14). Such prophetic pronouncements certainly substantiate Amos' major message of judgment and destruction for Israel. The fall of Israel to Assyria in 722 B.C. only served to confirm that "the-end-is-near" prophetic message of gloom from Amos was true.

Was there no future for Israel, no possibility of restoration that Amos could offer? A glimmer of hope appears at the very end of the book (9:11-15). Speaking on behalf of God, Amos declared: "I will restore the fortunes of my people Israel, and they shall rebuild the ruined cities and inhabit them" (9:14).

Is this the same prophet who earlier proclaimed such a harsh "no-hope-Israel-will-never-rise-again" message? Some scholars say "no" and attribute 9:11-15 to the work of a later editor, possibly a disciple of Amos. Other scholars insist that 9:11-15 is authentic Amos. Indeed, this final passage does not deny that God's judgment happened. It does, however, hold open the possibility that this God for whom Amos spoke could somehow (even in ways that from a human perspective seemed contradictorily mysterious) fashion a new start from an old ending. A God who could instill a spirit of "possibility" into a seemingly impossible situation. A God who in the midst of a "preach-judgment-and-destruction" ministry could somehow still have for Amos a word of hope.

The Structure of the Book

The book of Amos is composed of two major parts: the words of Amos (chaps. 1–6) and the visions of Amos (chaps. 7–9). As we explore the "words" section, we will gain a sampling of Amos' preaching, including one full-length sermon (1:3–2:16) as well as excerpts from other prophetic messages that Amos proclaimed. We will discover that Amos employed quite a bit of variety in his preaching. Although he sometimes followed standard formulas in structuring his sermons (for example, the use of the messenger formula in chapters 1 and 2), his messages were not limited to a stereotypical or predictable pattern. He also used various other forms and ingredients in his sermons including a funeral dirge (5:2), doxologies (4:13; 5:8-9), woes (5:18; 6:1, 4), and rhetorical questions (3:3-8).

Preacher Amos did not always have "three points and a poem"! Yet, he did manage to hammer home at least one point per message, and his sermons—as was characteristic of most Hebrew prophetic proclamation—were more poetic than narrative in nature. His audience certainly did not like or agree with the content of his preaching, but his skill in using a variety of sermon structures (as well as his evident gifts as a speaker) helped assure that the "words of Amos" would be heard.

Chapters 7–9, the second major part of the book of Amos, record five visions that Amos experienced (7:1-3; 7:4-6; 7:7-9; 8:1-3; 9:1-4). Indeed, the book of Amos contains more visions than any other prophetic book in the Old Testament. Amos' visions were highly intense, personal encounters with God through which Amos became convinced of Israel's pending doom. We do not know precisely when he "saw" these visions. Perhaps these visions occurred during his shepherding days in Judah when he received God's call to journey North to Israel and preach. Maybe the visions he experienced were part of his initial, or even his ongoing, call process. Whenever, or even however, such visions occurred, they provided Amos with the message of judgment and doom that he was to proclaim.

Couched within the visions section of Amos are two significant "non-visionary" passages. One is the classic confrontation between Amos and Amaziah, the professional priest of the royal sanctuary at Bethel (7:10-17). In the second passage (9:11-15), Amos provides a hint of hope in an otherwise "anything-but-hopeful" book. Whether the work of a later editor or the preaching of Amos himself, this passage allows the book of Amos as we have it to conclude with the mention of hope.

The Formulation of the Book

The book of Amos did not just drop out of heaven around 760 B.C., completely intact as we now have it. Neither did Amos copy it verbatim as he passively sat someplace listening to God verbally dictate all nine chapters. Rather, the book of Amos is the inspired record of the messages that Amos preached and the visions he experienced.

How did this divinely inspired record take shape? How did it come to be in its present form? It all began with God calling Amos, the layman shepherd-farmer, to go North and preach to Israel. Perhaps the calling of Amos came through some or all of the visions he experienced.

Amos responded to the divine call, went North, and started preaching. His sermons, which form the basis of the book named after him, were delivered orally. Amos probably preached without notes. There were no written manuscripts of his sermons. Neither did someone record on tape or paper his messages as soon as he spoke them.

How, then, were the divinely inspired words of Amos preserved? The messages were kept alive through oral transmission. Though not many Israelites liked the messages of Amos, they evidently remembered what Amos preached. Even Amaziah the priest gave an oral report about some of Amos' sermons to Jeroboam II (7:10-11). Quite probably Amos, like other prophets and teachers, had disciples who traveled with him and preserved his

messages by orally repeating and retelling them time and
time again.

How long the "book" of Amos remained in this
oral, fluid-like state is not precisely known. The words of
Amos were not likely committed to writing until after he
was "kicked out" of Israel and returned to Judah. Back
home, Amos' "northern" messages continued to "live" orally for awhile. Perhaps God used some crisis such as the fall
of Samaria in 722 B.C., or even the advancing age or
approaching death of Amos to inspire Amos' disciples or
even Amos himself to record Amos' preaching and visions
in written form.

At this juncture, as the oral tradition was committed
to writing, the book was probably arranged into its two
major parts: the words section and the visions section respectively. The task of this editor/compiler (whether it was
Amos or one or more of his disciples) was to sift through
the oral records of Amos' preaching and visions and to ar-
range them in a manner that would make sense to readers
and hearers of the book. James Limburg speculates about
the nature of this editorial work as follows:

> A careful reading indicates that considerable
> thought has gone into the collecting, selecting,
> and editing of the "words of Amos" (1:1) as they
> are gathered here. Some of the prophet's sayings
> were no doubt eliminated. Others were supple-
> mented, to make them more suitable for the new
> audiences they would address. At certain points
> we hear remarks such as a modern teacher or
> commentator might make (3:7; 5:13). At others,
> the editor has inserted fragments of hymnic
> material (4:13; 5:8-9; 9:5-6).

All of this editorial work was done with the aim
of making the words of the prophet from Tekoa
more accessible to those who would hear them
as they were read before the gathered community of believers. The fact that 1:1 mentions the
king of Judah before the king of Israel suggests
that this editing was done in Judah, after the fall
of Israel in 722 B.C. had validated such prophetic
words as 7:17.[2]

Whatever (or even whenever) the precise nature of the editorial process that resulted in the formation of the book as
we have it today, we need to realize its importance. Indeed,
we can argue that God was no less involved in the structuring and editing of the book of Amos than the Lord was
involved in the call, the visions, and the preaching of Amos
upon which the book is based.

I have no doubt that God could have delivered the
book of Amos without utilizing human agents. Yet, how
grateful I am that God did work through people: through
the preaching ministry of Amos, through the disciples who
kept alive Amos' words and visions in via oral transmission, and through the editor(s) who compiled the book in
its final form. Understanding how people were actively
involved in the preaching and writing of Holy Scripture
helps contemporary believers to be more open and sensi-
tive as to how God can work through their lives today.

Questions for Reflection

1. What is the historical setting of the book of Amos?

2. How does the phrase "It was the best of times; it was the worst of times" apply to the northern kingdom of Amos' day?

3. What was Amos' vocation?

4. What was the basic message proclaimed by Amos?

5. How did the book of Amos come to be in its present form?

Notes

[1]Ralph L. Smith, "Amos," *The Broadman Bible Commentary* (Nashville: Broadman Press, 1972) 82.

[2]James Limburg, *Hosea-Micah*, "Interpretation: A Biblical Commentary for Teaching and Preaching" (Atlanta: John Knox Press, 1988) 81.

For Further Reading

Andersen, Francis I. and David Noel Freedman. "Amos: A New Translation with Introduction and Commentary," in *The Anchor Bible*, vol. 24A, Garden City NY: Doubleday & Company, Inc., 1980.

Anderson, Bernhard W. *Understanding The Old Testament*. 2d ed. Englewood Cliffs NJ: Prentice-Hall, Inc., 1966.

Claypool, John. *Glad Reunion: Meeting Ourselves in the Lives of Bible Men and Women*. Waco: Word Books, 1985.

Fosbroke, Hugell E.W. "The Book of Amos," *The Interpreter's Bible*, VI: 761-853. New York: Abingdon Press, 1956.

Limburg, James. *Hosea-Micah*. Interpretation: A Biblical Commentary for Teaching and Preaching. Atlanta: John Knox Press, 1988.

Martin-Achard, R. and S. Paul Re'emi. *Amos & Lamentations: God's People in Crisis*. International Theological Commentary. Edinburgh: The Handsel Press LTD, 1984.

Mays, James Luther. *Amos*. The Old Testament Library. Philadelphia: The Westminster Press, 1974.

Peterson, Eugene H. *Working The Angles: The Shape of Pastoral Authority*. Grand Rapids MI: Eerdmans, 1987.

Rust, Eric C. *Covenant and Hope*. Waco: Word Books, 1972.

Shelley, John C. "Amos," *Mercer Commentary on the Bible*, 743-55. Macon GA: Mercer University Press, 1995.

Shoemaker, H. Stephen. *The Jekyll & Hyde Syndrome*. Nashville: Broadman Press, 1987.

Smith, Ralph L. "Amos," *The Broadman Bible Commentary* ,
       VII: 81-141. Nashville: Broadman Press, 1972
Stuart, Douglas. *Hosea-Jonah,* in Word Biblical Commentary,
       Vol. 31. Waco: Word Books, 1987.
Von Rad, Gerhard. *The Message of the Prophets*. Trans. D. M.
       G. Stalker. New York: Harper and Row Publishers,
       1967.
West, James King. *Introduction to the Old Testament*. 2d ed.
       New York: Macmillan Publishing Co., Inc., 1981.

Chapter 1

A Sermon against Surrounding Nations (and Israel, too!)

1:3-2:16

> When a preacher in a sermon
> > Speaks about the world of sin,
> As he tries hard to arouse us
> > From the lethargy we're in,
> We think, "Oh, I knew they'd get it;
> > They deserve it, glory be.
> He must mean the other fellow.
> > He can't possibly mean me!"
> > > —Anonymous

Have you ever noticed how we like to hear about the faults of others? Though we might never admit it, we are often secretly pleased when we find out about someone else "sinning" or "getting caught." (Gossip seldom consists of the good things people do!) Granted, this tendency to delight clandestinely (if not openly) in the sins and shortcomings of others does not speak well of us. Yet it is part of us, unbecoming though it may be.

Amos evidently recognized this unbecoming aspect of human nature and utilized it to call attention to a sermon he preached. Recall the prophetic task of Amos for just a moment. His assignment was to leave the friendly confines of his Judean homeland in the South and travel North to Israel where he was to preach a message of judgment against the Israelites. Certainly cognizant of the fact that the Israelites would not be lining up to hear his "doom and gloom" message about their own sins, Amos knew he needed an entree into Israel, something that would provide him with the opportunity to proclaim his divinely mandated message. That something turned out to be this propensity of people to be attracted to and even to take pleasure in hearing about the sins and shortcomings of others.

We can imagine Amos in Samaria, the capital city of Israel, mingling with the people in the marketplace. Perhaps it was a festival day when many more folks than usual would be in the capital city that tended to draw crowds of people even during normal non-holiday times. Suddenly a booming voice rose above the noisy chatter and clatter of the marketplace. It was the voice of Amos. After taking a deep breath and uplifting a silent prayer for courage, the prophet Amos from Judah had started to preach:

> "Thus says the Lord," he proclaims. "For three transgressions of Damascus (the capital of Syria) and for four I will not revoke the punishment. . . . I will send a fire on the house of Hazael (a dynasty of Syrian kings). . . . I will break the gate bars of Damascus . . . and the people of Aram (another name for Syria) shall go into exile to Kir, says the Lord." (1:3-5)

The preaching against Syria, one of Israel's age-old enemies, quickly drew a crowd. The growing Israelite audience started to get "caught up" in the sermon and even became overtly responsive:

> That's right, Amos. Let those Syrians have it. It's high time somebody called those people from Aram to task. Amen. Those pagans up there in Damascus don't even worship the Lord. They serve a bunch of false gods. No wonder they treat others so cruelly and unjustly. Let'em have it, Amos. That's right. Amen. Preach on.

And preach on Amos did! Having "hooked" his audience by calling attention to and condemning the people of Syria for their sins, Amos set the hook even deeper by sermonically moving from one surrounding nation to another. From Syria in the Northeast to Philistia in the Southwest to Tyre in the Northwest to Moab and Edom in the Southeast, Amos moved. The prophet crisscrossed Israel as it were with indictments and divine judgments against Israel's neighbors.

As Amos identified the sin of each neighboring people and pronounced God's subsequent judgment, the interest of his ever-growing Israelite audience increased, and the fervor with which they encouraged Amos intensified. "Amen, brother Amos. Tell it like it is. God's gonna give them what they deserve. Preach on."

So Amos continued to preach. He next moved even closer to the northern kingdom by directing his fiery rhetoric against Judah. When the sermon began focusing on Israel's rival southern neighbors, the Israelite audience must have been especially receptive and responsive. Although Judah worshiped the right God, Judean religion (at least from the northern perspective of the Israelites) was not very refined. After all, they might have reasoned, "What can you expect from a bunch of southerners?" Even Amos himself recognized the transgressions of his own native Judah, and the accolades for Amos continued:

> What a great job, Amos! Thanks for the terrific message. You really stepped on their toes today. You're such a gifted preacher. Keep up the good work. We look forward to hearing you preach again real soon.

Amos was not finished preaching, however. You might say that he was just warming up! Before the people could gather up their belongings and start to leave, Amos pulled a real shocker: he started preaching against Israel. In fact, Amos really let Israel have it that day, calling attention not just to one sin as had been his pattern in dealing with the other nations, but specifying an entire list of sins for which Israel would be punished.

Not just punished, but destroyed. The response of Amos' shockingly surprised audience changed as quickly as Amos could declare: "And you, O Israel, have sinned too! You also will reap God's judgment." Again, we can imagine the feedback from the people:

> Wait a minute, Amos. You've stopped preaching and gone to meddlin'. You don't know what you're talking about.
> Israel be destroyed? You're mistaken, man. We're God's chosen people, remember? Just look around Amos. Things are going great under Jeroboam II. God is really blessing us right now. Why pretty soon when the "day of the Lord" arrives, we're going to be elevated to

the status of being the number one nation in all
the world!

So get a grip, Amos. You're talking
crazy. Maybe you've been out in the sun with
the sheep for too long. Chill out! Either tone
down the rhetoric, or shut up and go back home
to Judah. We don't need your kind of preaching
around here!"

For awhile at least, however, Israel heard Amos'
"kind of preaching." In Amos 1:3–2:16, we have a record of
what might be regarded as a "full-length-Amos-kind-of-
preaching" sermon. Take a closer look.

The Pattern

We begin by noting that the sermon, though full and complete, is not especially lengthy. The scholar James Limburg
found that the entire sermon can be read aloud in Hebrew
in just ten minutes. Even when allowing for interruptions
(especially the "amens" as well as the protests of the
crowd), the actual delivery of this sermon would probably
encompass no more than twelve minutes.[1]

Though short in length, this sermon that launches
the book of Amos must have been powerful in presentation. The sermon itself consists of eight oracles or "sermon
points," if you will. (The oracle was the basic literary unit
of Hebrew prophecy, often a brief, poetic declaration.) Each
of these eight "sermon points" or oracles was actually an
indictment against one of eight different nations.

The first six indictments were directed against six
small nations that surrounded Israel: Syria (1:3-5), Philistia

(1:6-8), Phoenicia (1:9-10), Edom (1:11-12), Ammon (1:13-15), and Moab (2:1-3). The seventh indictment was directed against Judah (2:4-5). Amos concluded his sermon by dealing (in a much more expansive fashion) with a stinging indictment against Israel (2:6-16). Each of these eight oracles is cast in a stereotyped pattern that includes the following elements.

Messenger Formula: "Thus says the Lord"
(1:3, 6, 9, 11, 13; 2:1, 4, 6)

Before the invention of writing, messages were often relayed by a messenger. Kings, for example, would often send their trusted servants to other kings or monarchs in order to deliver a crucial message. As was universally recognized, the authority of the message lay with the sender (king) and not with the messenger or emissary. This fact helps explain why lone messengers traveling to enemy territory were not killed even when delivering an unfavorable or hostile message. The message was regarded as originating with the sender (king) rather than the messenger. Messengers were granted a type of diplomatic immunity that freed them to deliver accurately the message of the sender whom they represented.

The messenger formula "Thus says the Lord," which was frequently used by various Old Testament prophets, undoubtedly originated from this context. This phrase helps us understand why prophets could deliver harsh, judgmental messages to kings and nations without being executed (2 Sam 12; Amos 7:10-12). When a prophet prefaced his remarks with "Thus says the Lord," he was perceived as delivering a message from (and under the authority of) God!

Indictment Formula: "For three transgressions of ___and for four, I will not revoke the punishment."

The numbers in this indictment formula are not to be taken literally but should be regarded symbolically. "Three" stands for enough, while "four" in this context can be rendered "more than enough." In Amos' view, the sin of a nation or society could reach a "saturation point" beyond which the Lord would not allow matters to continue without pronouncing judgment on that society. The number "three" represents the saturation point; the number "four" represents the breaking point, thus ensuring God's judgment.[2]

"For three transgressions . . . and for four" actually refers to a multitude of sins. Yet, for the purposes of this sermon, Amos, except in his treatment of Israel, charged each of the nations with one specific crime. Also noteworthy is the Hebrew word *pesha* that Amos used in this phrase. Translated as "transgressions," *pesha* indicates that the nations under indictment were in a state of rebellion against the God of Israel.

How interesting that even when non-Israelite nations were accused of mistreating other non-Israelite nations (in 2:1-3, where Moab is condemned for committing crimes against Edom), they were still held accountable for being in rebellion against Israel's God. This God of Israel, then, was certainly not considered just a national deity, but the Lord God of the universe who was actively involved in the affairs of other nations, even those nations (such as Syria and Philistia) who were regarded as being among the worst enemies of Israel.

Specification of Crime: "Because they have . . ."

Amos utilized the phrase "because they have . . ." to specify one particular sin for which each nation, with the excep-
tion of Israel, was condemned. Amos dealt with Israel in an
expansive manner (2:6-16) and delineated a number of specific sins in the process. The specific transgressions for
which the six surrounding nations were accused all dealt
with crimes committed during war. Amos' accusation
against Judah was different. Rather than castigating his
own nation for a war crime, Amos enumerated Judah's
wrongdoing by declaring "because they have rejected the
law of the Lord, and have not kept his statutes" (2:4).

**Judgment Formula: "So I will send a fire upon ____ and it
shall devour the strongholds of ____."**

Amos used the "fill-in-the-blank" formula seven times (1:4,
7, 10, 12, 14; 2:2, 5) in the pronouncing of judgment. The
fire that the Lord (the divine "I") would send refers to the
fire of warfare, both in terms of warfare's general destruction and also in regard to the fires that invading armies
would set as they marched upon a city.

Concluding Formula: ". . . says the Lord"

The phrase ". . . says the Lord" appears at the end of most
of the oracles or "sermon points" (1:5, 8, 15; 2:3, 11, 16).
Such an ending was a strong reminder to those who heard
Amos that the pronounced judgment on the respective nations was God's judgment. As God's messenger, Amos was
delivering a message from God.

The southern preacher effectively used this stereotyped pattern to deliver a highly charged sermon that commanded the attention of his northern listening audience.
Delineating and denouncing the sins of others, especially
one's neighboring enemies and rivals, all but guaranteed a
receptive congregation. What exactly did Amos say about
each of Israel's surrounding neighbors? What specific sin
did he single out in his diatribe against each nation? Keeping in mind the stereotyped pattern he used, take a closer
look at each of the oracles (sermon points or movements if
you will) in this brilliantly constructed and skillfully delivered "eight-point" sermon.

Oracles against Surrounding Foreign Nations (1:3–2:3)

The Oracle against Syria (1:3-5)

Damascus, the capital city of Syria (biblical Aram), was
used by Amos in 1:3-5 to represent the nation Syria. Each
of the first six nations in Amos' sermon were found guilty
of some type of war crime. The sin for which Syria was
singled out occurred in the aftermath of an earlier war—
actually a border clash—with Israel during which Syria had
captured Gilead, a part of Israel's territory east of the
Jordan River. By the time of Amos' sermon, Israel had
recaptured two Gilead cities, Lo-debar and Karnaim (6:13).
    Perhaps to our surprise, Amos did not condemn
Damascus/Syria for going to war against Israel in the
struggle to occupy Gilead. Rather, Syria was prophetically
reprimanded for its cruel treatment of the people of Gilead
whom it captured. Amos expressed Syria's inhumane crime

in these words: "because they have threshed Gilead with threshing sledges of iron" (1:4).

If taken literally, this phrase means that the Syrians dragged some type of heavy threshing sled over the bodies of Gilead captives. Such a sledge was probably a cart or sled-like vehicle that had wheels or runners into which iron spikes had been driven. One can only imagine the result of dragging such an implement over the body of a human being! Even if this phrase from Amos 1:4 is interpreted symbolically, it still portrays the cruel treatment that Syria enacted upon prisoners of war.

The mention of the house of Hazael in 1:4 refers to a royal dynasty of Syrian kings established in 842 B.C. by King Hazael. According to 2 Kings 8:7-13, Ben-hadad was part of this Syrian dynasty. The Valley of Aven and Beth-eden are evidently names of places in the Syria (Aram) of Amos' day that we can no longer identify.

Amos' pronouncement of the divine punishment that awaited Syria certainly caused no sorrow on the part of his Israelite audience. Since Syria was one of Israel's oldest enemies, an Isralite audience would undoubtedly have cheered (or at least satisfyingly smiled) upon hearing that Syria was about to receive a divine sentence for its sin. And the sentence? The nation would be engulfed by the fires of war, the capital city of Damascus would fall, and the inhabitants of Syria would be sent into exile (1:4-5). The reality of this judgment became evident just a few years later when in 732 B.C. Damascus was overthrown by Assyria under the leadership of Tiglath-Pileser III.

Notice that God is portrayed in these verses as the divine judge who seeks justice for a defenseless segment of the human population (in this case, the Gileadites who were prisoners of war). Seeking and demanding justice for the defenseless, the poor, and the little ones is a major theme to which God via Amos returned.

The Oracle against Philistia (1:6-8)

From Syria in the Northeast, Amos moved diagonally to the Southwest where he preached against another long-standing enemy of Israel, the Philistines (also known as the sea peoples). Four particular Philistine cities are mentioned in this oracle/sermon point: Gaza, Ashdod, Ashkelon, and Ekron. Gaza is singled out as the city that was used to "fill in the blanks" of Amos' stereotyped pattern (1:6-7). Gaza was actually representative of all the Philistine cities and citizens, however.

The Philistines were condemned particularly for engaging in slave trade. As Amos expressed the matter, "because they carried into exile entire communities, to hand them over to Edom" (1:6). Slave traffic with Edom— the capturing and selling of "entire communities" of people for material gain—was the sin that went beyond the "for-three-transgressions-and-for-four" saturation point, assuring God's judgment on Philistia. And the divine judgment? God would send fire (war) upon the Philistine people until "the last remnant" of the Philistines had "perished" (1:7-8).

The Oracle against Phoenicia/ Tyre (1:9-10)

From Gaza/Philistia in the Southwest, Amos sermonically moved Northwest up the Mediterranean coast to focus on the particular sin of Tyre, the chief city of the Phoenicians during his day. The city was singled out for condemnation because of the same transgression for which Gaza/Philistia had just been accused—namely, engaging in slave trade

with Edom. As Amos declared, "because they [Tyre] delivered entire communities over to Edom" (1:9b). This was no
small-scale operation, but the deportation of enormous
numbers of people (even entire communities) into slavery.

In condemning Tyre's crime of selling human beings
for profit, Amos added an additional word. In the process
of selling slaves to Edom, Tyre had also broken a
"covenant of kinship" (1:9c). Although this betrayed
covenant partner is not explicitly identified in the scripture,
the offended party from whom people were sold into
slavery could very well have been Israel. Indeed, the
"covenant of kinship" reference (1:9c) could point to the
friendly relationships that had been established between
Israel and Tyre (1 Kgs 5:12; 9:13; 16:30ff). Not only did Tyre
profit materially from selling people, it also broke a
covenant agreement with another nation, presumably
Israel. For its punishment, Tyre received the same sentence
as the other surrounding nations had received: the fiery
destruction of warfare (1:10; 1:4, 7, 12, 14; 2:2, 5).

The Oracle against Edom (1:11-12)

Amos next turned to the southeast in order to preach
against Edom. The attentive eighth-century B.C. listener and
certainly today's perceptive reader would notice that Amos
—through the progression of his sermon points or oracles—
figuratively crisscrossed Israel two times: from northeast
Syria to southwest Philistia to northwest Phoenicia and
then to the Southeast where he dealt respectively with
Edom (1:11-12), Ammon (1:13-15), and Moab (2:1-3). A
rough diagram of the movement of Amos' sermon might
look something like the following illustration.

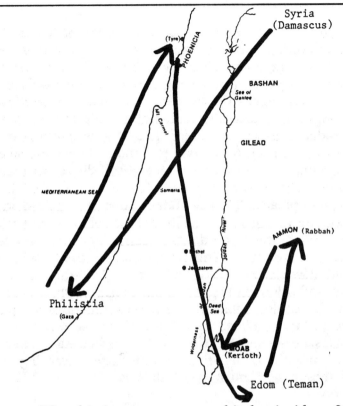

Was this just some geographical coincidence? Or was there some purpose in this geographical crisscrossing? Does this geographical pattern not at least imply that the Lord is a universal God who is concerned not only with Israel but with all nations in all directions who are in some way (geographically, figuratively, or otherwise) "connected" to Israel? Does not Amos' pattern of crisscrossing Israel in order to deal with the sins of other nations strongly suggest that Israel might have had a sin or two with which it needed to deal?

Yet, at this point in the sermon, the people in the Israelite audience seemed oblivious to any possible short-comings that they themselves might have had, so enthralled were they in hearing Amos denounce the sins of others. Still apparently unaware that Amos was skillfully moving toward a condemnation of and a pronouncement of God's judgment against their own sins, the Israelites encouraged Amos to "preach on" and "let'em have it" as the prophet began to focus on the sins of the southeastern nations of Edom, Ammon, and Moab.

In preaching against Edom, Amos was taking on a people who were distant relatives of Israel. The Edomites, in fact, were the descendants of Esau (Gen 36:1-43). Ever since the days and events represented by the Jacob-Esau stories (Gen 25:19-34; 27:1–33:20), the relationship between Israel and Edom had been strained at best (Num 20:14-21) and often could only be characterized as hateful and bellig-erent (1 Sam 14:47; 2 Sam 8:13-14). There was certainly no love lost between these two nations. So when Amos "lit in" to Edom with his "hell-fire-and-brimstone" preaching, the Israelites surely must have cheered and voiced their approval.

Amos had already cited Edom as being a partner of both Gaza/Philistia and Tyre/Phoenicia in large-scale slave trading (1:6, 9). Curiously, however, the sin that Amos singled out in his denunciation of Edom was not slavery but constant warfare against "his brother" (1:11). Because of Israel's kinship to Edom and the longstanding enmity and fighting between the two nations, a good case could be made for identifying this "brother whom Edom angrily pur-sued with the sword" as Israel. Whether the target of this hateful warfare was Israel or some other related nation, Edom's sin was not only the pursuit of war but the

zealous, perpetual anger with which such familial warfare
was pursued!

Edom replaced the compassion that should characterize "brothers," and "sisters," and "family" members with
a passion for ongoing hatred and even destructive conduct.
Or as Amos expressed the matter,

> He [Edom] pursued his brother with the sword
> and cast off all pity; he maintained his anger
> perpetually, and kept his wrath forever. (1:11)

Perhaps you personally do not know any brothers,
sisters, or kinfolks who are actually involved in a literal,
physical war with one another. But don't all of us know of
brothers who maintain ever-present anger toward and
hatred for each other? Don't all of us know of sisters, husbands and wives, children and parents, church members,
and even denominational leaders who are continuously
mad at and constantly fighting with other family members?
Aren't such people guilty of the sin of Edom? Don't such
persons in effect perpetuate a kind of ongoing war with
one another? Aren't we—more often than we care to admit
—guilty of this sin of Edom ourselves?

Teman was the chief city in the southern part of
Edom during the time of Amos. Bozrah was a major Edomite city in Edom's northern region. Both of these cities are
mentioned in verse 13 where the divine punishment against
Edom is recorded. Just as Teman and Bozrah encompassed
Edom geographically, so would the fires of warfare—God's
judgment against Edom—encompass and devour the entire
nation. This Edomite nation, who with ardent animosity
waged war continuously against others, would—in accordance with the divine timetable of judgment—become a

victim of war itself. Living by the sword leads to death by the sword.

The Oracle against Ammon (1:13-15)

The Ammonites were also related to Israel. According to Genesis 19:30-38, the Ammonites (and Moabites for that matter) were descendants of Lot, the nephew of Abraham. The sin that pushed Ammon beyond the Lord's "for-three-transgressions-and-for-four" saturation point of tolerance was a border war initiated by the Ammonites in order to expand their territory northward into Gilead.

Even more reprehensible than the warfare itself was the treatment by victorious Ammonites to the pregnant women in Gilead. They ripped open their wombs, killing not only the defenseless women but simultaneously blotting out the lives of those who should have been the next generation! This horrible practice was politically motivated (especially in border wars) as it provided the captors with a means—ghastly though it was—of keeping control of a region by the terror it imposed and the reduced residential population it caused.

Like the punishment to be imposed on the other nations surrounding Israel, Ammon's divine sentence would be destruction by the fires of war (1:14a). The motif of exile previously mentioned in the judgment pronounced against Syria (1:5) once again appeared (1:15). Amos also employed two new features in his description of God's impending judgment on Ammon: the battle or war-cry (1:14b) that the attacking army would shout as they defeated their Ammonite victims (Jer 4:19; Amos 2:2) and the image of a tempest or whirlwind (1:14a) indicating the fury with which divine judgment on Ammon would be unleashed (Jer 23:19; Ezek

13:13). These newly introduced features underscore the indignation of God that was ignited whenever innocent and defenseless persons of a society (in this case the captive pregnant women of Gilead) were mistreated and/or harmed.

The Oracle against Moab (2:1-3)

Amos remained in the southeast quadrant of his geographical sermon structure as he finished the "foreign" oracles portion of his sermon. Like the Ammonites, the Moabites were also descendants of Lot (Gen 19:30-38) and, consequently, related to Israel. The specific sin for which Moab was denounced was that of having "burned" to lime the bones of the king of Edom (2:1). While Amos' original audience was evidently well-aware of this wrongful action, the precise nature or date of Moab's crime is no longer known by us. Some type of sacrilegious action was apparently taken by the Moabites that involved the burning of the remains of an Edomite king.

Was the Edomite king burned alive? Or did the Moabites burn the king's body after he died by some other means but prior to his burial? Or could it be that Moab's hatred for Edom was so intense that the body of the already buried king was exhumed and then burned?

Whatever the precise nature of the deed, it was regarded as an act of shameful profanation. Moab's punishment for this crime would be death and destruction via war. Just as Moab burned and destroyed the bones of the Edomite king, so would Moab be "burned" and destroyed by the fiery flames of war. Amos made Moab's coming judgment by warfare seem even more vivid by once again mentioning the shouting or battle-cry of war (2:2; 1:14b) and by referring to the bugle or trumpet that was utilized in warfare.

Most remarkably, the crime that God condemned did not directly involve Israel. It was the crime of one foreign nation, Moab, against another foreign nation, Edom. Yet, Amos still believed that such a crime was nonetheless a crime and sin against Yahweh, Israel's God. Talk about the universal nature of God—this is it! Amos was declaring that the Lord cared when nations mistreated each other whether Israel was involved or not.

As demonstrated by the geographical structuring of his sermon and as further demonstrated through God's condemnation of Moab for its crime against the Edomite king, Amos showed that the Lord whom he served was very concerned about and involved with non-Israelite nations. The God of Amos would even hold these foreign nations accountable for their actions and judge them when their sins exceeded the saturation point. This God certainly was (and is) the Lord of the universe!

With his delineation of Moab's sin and impending punishment, Amos completed the foreign nations section of his sermon. He crisscrossed Israel twice, moving from northeast (Syria) to southwest (Philistia) to northwest (Phoenicia) to southeast (Edom, Ammon, and Moab). He progressed from dealing with two of Israel's long standing enemies (the Syrians and the Philistines) to a traditionally more "Israelite-friendly" people (Tyre/Phoenicia) to a group of kinship nations (Edom, Ammon, and Moab).[3] Amos cunningly and almost clandestinely moved another step closer to his Israelite audience as he turned to preach against Judah.

The Oracle against Judah
(2:4-5)

We can imagine that Amos' Israelite hearers, who were already "really getting into" the sermon, grew even more appreciative and responsive as Amos preached against his own people, Judah. Surely the Israelites' direct kinship to Judah with whom they had once been united as a nation only served to heighten the northern kingdom's endorsement of anyone who would point out the shortcomings of her southern neighbor-kinfolks. As we listen to Amos' proclamation of God's judgment against Judah, we must not forget the intense North-South rivalry that motivated Israel to encourage Amos to "preach on":

> Amen, Amos. Now you're really preachin'. Finally, a southern prophet is saying what we have long known to be true—that Judah needs to repent. We're a much more quality nation without Judah.
>
> Tell it like it is, Amos. Judah does worship the right God, but her citizens continuously fail to do the right thing and (unlike us) to live the right way.
>
> What a daring and dynamic preacher you are, Amos! Keep on telling the people of Judah what they're doing wrong. Maybe one day they'll see the light and become more like us. Preach on!

Unlike the particular sin for which each of the preceding nations was condemned, the sin for which Judah was judged in Amos' sermon was not related to war crimes. Instead, the people of Judah were denounced by preacher Amos "because they have rejected the law of the Lord and have not kept his statutes" (2:4). By this, Amos probably meant that his Hebrew kinfolks were not following the instruction and teaching of God as was communicated to them through their priests. In other words, the people of Judah were not keeping the Lord's commandments. Their sin was that of failing to put their religion into daily practices.

The people of Judah were judged differently than the surrounding foreign nations because they had a different relationship with the divine judge. They (along with Israel) were part of God's covenant people. Yet, like God's covenant people, they had not been living. They were led astray by their own disobedience and inclination to follow the negative example of their ancestors who also failed to follow God's laws (2:4c).

Like the surrounding foreign nations, Judah would be punished by God through the fiery ravages of war (2:5). Strangely, exile was not mentioned as part of Judah's punishment; it had been previously included in God's judgment on some of the other nations (1:5, 15) and had played such a prominent role nearly two centuries later (597 and 587 B.C.) when the judgment of both destructive warfare in and exile for Judah was realized.

Blinded to the reality that Israel was even more guilty of similar sins, the Israelites must have gleefully agreed with Amos' strong preaching against Judah. Following his treatment of Judah, Amos' audience must have also thought that Amos' sermon was finished. If you and I had been living in that culture and had been present in that eighth-century B.C. audience, we would have thought that as well. With the oracle on Judah, the number of nations against whom Amos preached reached seven, a number that in biblical times was quite frequently used to refer to completeness (Gen 1:1–2:3; Lev 26:18, 21, 24; Matt 18:21-22; Luke 17:4).[4]

     Sermon point number seven on Judah had been preached. The message was complete. The sermon was over. Preacher Amos had done an outstanding job. It was time to go home. At this point Amos pulled a real surprise, however. He was not finished preaching. Why, he had more than seven points! Having kept his audience's attention by preaching "around" Israel and condemning the sins of everybody else, the southern prophet Amos dared to do the unthinkable: he started preaching against the sins of Israel!

The Oracle against Israel
(2:6-16)

Before his stunned audience could shout or leave in protest, Amos commenced preaching to and against his Israelite congregation. The once responsive crowd grew strangely silent as Amos inserted the name of Israel into the stereotyped pattern with which he had pronounced judgment against the previous seven nations: "Thus says the Lord: For three transgresions of Israel, and for four, I will not revoke the punishment; because . . ." (2:6).

     Never in their wildest dreams did the Israelites imagine that the name of their nation would appear in Amos' "fill-in-the-blank" formula. Yet, here it was for all to hear (and later to see)—the name, their name, Israel! How easy (and even delightful) it had been to hear about the sins of all the nations surrounding them! But how difficult (and even impossible) to hear about the sins of their own nation! Like so many people (this writer and contemporary readers included), Israel saw the sins of others with 20/20 vision. Yet, the nation was all but blind when it came to seeing its own sins.

Who did this southerner Amos think he was anyway? Using smooth and clever rhetoric to trick them into listening to his sermon, knowing all the while that his real intent was to preach against them! And preach against them Amos did—even harder and more fervently than he preached against the other nations. Rather than identifying and denouncing just one particular Israelite sin as had been his pattern in dealing with the other countries, Amos cited a whole catalogue of Israelite transgressions (2:6-8). It was as if the prophet wanted to linger on the sins of his northern congregation, and linger long on the sins of Israel Amos did.

The Current Sins of Israel (2:6-8)

Which sins of Israel did Amos delineate and proclaim judgment against in this final and climactic part of his masterfully ingenious sermon? Scholars debate the actual number of Israelite sins that Amos enumerated, but for our purposes we will offer a brief survey of several of Israel's top sins.

(1) Selling the righteous in slavery. Israel was guilty of "selling the righteous for silver" (1:6). Amos charged his northern kinsfolk with engaging in the sin of slave trading just as he had previously condemned Philistia and Phoenicia for the same practice. (How ironic that Israel had encouraged Amos to castigate these two nations for the sin

of slavery while somehow failing to acknowledge that their participation in the sale of human beings for monetary gain was their sin, too!) While acknowledging slavery as an institution, Israel's law codes (Exod 21:2-11; Deut 15:12-18) did seek to put controls on slavery. Selling righteous people for sheer profit was not in keeping with the law codes.

The "righteous" who were sold into slavery were the honest, often poor, Israelite citizens who simply tried to do what was right. More specifically, the term "righteous" (*tsaddiq*) denotes the innocent as opposed to the guilty party in "a legal process, the man in the right whom the court should vindicate."[5] As Amos would soon point out, the judicial system favored the rich often at the expense of the innocent-righteous (5:10, 12, 15). Slave trading was practiced in Israel because making money (silver) was more important than helping poor people who were righteous.

(2) Confiscating the property of the poor. Selling "the needy for a pair of sandals" (2:6b) parallels the preceding "selling the righteous for silver" and consequently refers to the same basic crime of selling the innocent and oppressed into slavery. The phrase "a pair of sandals" could simply mean "a very little" (Gen 14:23), in which case some Israelites placed very little value on the lives of fellow Israelites. There is another possible dimension to this particular sin of Israel, however.

People in the ancient Near East had a custom of calling for the use of sandals in the transaction of land (Ruth 4:7). The buyer of property would "seal the deal," not with a handshake but by giving a sandal(s) to the seller. "Selling the needy for a pair of sandals" could be Amos' way of charging Israelite businessmen with confiscating the property of the needy, righteous Israelites who were sold into slavery. Israelites were not only making money in the slave trade of fellow Israelites; they were making a "steal" in the real estate market as well!

(3) Mistreating the poor. "Trampling the head of the poor into the dust of the earth" (2:7a) was Amos' image for the constant abuse that the poor of Israel suffered at the hands (and feet) of their wealthier Israelite neighbors. Remember that in the "best of times, worst of times" scenario of eighth-century B.C. Israel, the rich got richer while the poor became poorer. Far too often, the advancement of the rich came at the expense of those less fortunate. Almost without a second thought, many Israelites were "walking all over" the "poor" whom Amos also referred to as the "righteous," the "needy," and the "afflicted" (2:6-7).

(4) Corrupting justice. The "push-the-afflicted-out-of-the-way" in verse 7 is an idiom used to refer to the corruption of justice in the court system. Poorer Israelites found it all but impossible to get a "fair shake" in court because those who worked in the judicial and legal systems used their offices for personal gain (via bribery, favoritism, and other means) rather than for the administration of justice. Amos returned again and again to this theme of establishing justice in the law courts as well as in other realms of society (5:10, 12, 15, 24).

(5) Practicing immorality. Some commentators believe that the phrase "father and son go in to the same girl so that my holy name is profaned" (2:7b) refers to the sin of sacred prostitution (á lá Hosea). Although this explanation is possible, Amos did not employ the specific Hebrew term for sacred prostitute but instead used the much more neutral

term translated girl or maiden. A more probable interpretation is that this "girl" or maiden had been sold as a domestic slave because of her own family's poverty. The owner and his son demanded more from the girl than housework, however. Both had sexual relations with her, reducing her to an object rather than continuing to recognize her as a person. Such immoral activity was prohibited by Israelite law (Exod 21:7-11; Lev 25:39).

(6) Abusing debtors. The Israelite legal system allowed a creditor to require a debtor to provide some type of security such as a coat. This same legal system, however, provided some degree of protection for the debtor. For example, a coat held by a creditor as surety had to be returned by nightfall since it could be the only covering that a poor person had for protection from the cold (Exod 22:25-27).

Amos charged wealthy Israelite creditors with misusing garments held as security. "They lay themselves down beside every altar on garments taken in pledge" (2:8) suggests that the creditors not only failed to return such pledged garments as required by the law, but that such garments were even frequently taken to (and apparently left at) "church" where they were used as furnishings for the altar. In short, the Israelites furnished the "house of God" (their churches) with garments that belonged to and should have been returned to the poor. Just the hint of mistreating the poor in order to decorate the altar at church was anathema to Amos!

(7) Selfishly exploiting the poor under the guise of religion. The Israelite law code called for the restitution of certain crimes through the paying of fines (Deut 22:19; Exod 21:22). Since the poor were nearly always strapped for cash, their fines

could apparently be paid "in kind." Amos 2:8b portrays a situation in which a poor man had evidently paid his fine with wine that he produced. This "wine gained from fines" was rather lavishly and wastefully consumed in religious festivals and activities at church by rich worshipers who were more than capable of providing wine for the services from their own resources.

Something did not seem quite right about the use of poor people's "wines and fines" by rich parishioners in their church services. Amos declared that such exploitation of the poor under the guise of religion was not right. It was sinfully wrong. Yet, it was still another indication that many Israelites saw little if any connection between their worship of God on the one hand and their treatment of poor Israelites on the other.

The Past Blessings of God (2:9-12)

With his Israelite audience still reeling from his identification of their sins, Amos further demonstrated the guilt of the Israelites by adding a new weapon to his preaching arsenal: he recounted crucial moments in Israel's history when God had intervened and acted on Israel's behalf. Amos used this recital of God's mighty acts (Deut 26:5ff., Josh 24:2ff., and Ps 136) to show why Israel of all people should express gratitude for such divine intervention by living moral and ethical lifestyles. Yet, despite these momentous past blessings of God, Israel still refused to practice justice or do what was right.

The conquest: "I destroyed the Amorite before them" (2:9). The term Amorite and Canaanite are often used interchangeably to refer to the people who occupied the Promised Land prior to the Israelites. Speaking on God's behalf (notice the divine "I"), Amos reminded the Israelites that the conquest of Canaan was not their own doing. The Lord was the party responsible for Israel possessing the land. Israel, then, was living in a land that God had given to the nation. Yet, based on its sinful actions, Israel was not all that grateful for the promised land gift. Just as God had destroyed the Amorite, so too could Israel be destroyed.

The Exodus: "I brought you up out of the land of Egypt" (2:10a). Amos called attention to the Exodus, the pivotal event in Israel's salvation history. Again, notice the use of the "divine I" as Amos spoke for the Lord. "Surely recalling how God saved their people from Egyptian slavery will inspire them to practice righteous and ethical living," Amos reasoned. He reasoned incorrectly. As we shall see (3:1-2; 5:18-20), Israel believed that being God's people as a result of the exodus event meant privilege rather than responsibility.

The guidance in the wilderness: "I . . . led you forty years in the wilderness" (2:10b). The Lord did not just "save" Israel and then abandon it. Rather, God provided guidance and sustenance as the nation wandered and struggled through that long forty-year wilderness period prior to entrance into the Promised Land. Remembering how God had "been there" for them during the tough wilderness times should have motivated the Israelites to obey and follow God in the present—or so Amos thought. Again the prophet thought wrong.

Another allusion to the conquest: ". . . to possess the land of the Amorite" (2:10c). "The land of Canaan has not always been your land," Amos told his audience. "It is a gift of God. Use the gift wisely."

The sending of the prophets: "I raised up some of your children to be prophets" (2:11). The Lord did not withdraw from Israel once the Promised Land was possessed. God continued to relate to the Israelites through the calling and sending of prophets. Yet, Israel for the most part had not regarded the prophets as good gifts from God. As Amos soon discovered, Israel's historical and current response to the prophets was one of rejection: "You shall not prophesy" (2:12b; 7:13-16; Isa 30:10-11; Jer 11:21; Micah 2:6).

The gift of Nazirites: "I raised up . . . some of your youths to be nazirites" (2:11b). Along with the prophets, God also called nazirites to be spiritual leaders among Israel. Nazirites were those males and females in Israel who felt led to be especially devoted to God. The term Nazirites is from a Hebrew verb root (*nzr*) meaning "to dedicate or to consecrate" and is related to another Hebrew verb (*ndr*) meaning "to vow." One assumed the role of a Nazirite by taking some specific vows of separation and abstinence. According to Numbers 6:1-8, there were three such vows: (1) to abstain from alcoholic beverages, (2) to abstain from cutting the hair (as long hair was a visual reminder of consecration to God), and (3) to avoid any contact with a corpse that would make them ritually unclean.

"But you made the Nazirites drink wine" (2:12), was Amos' way of declaring that the Israelites not only rejected God's gift of these dedicated, spiritual leaders. The influence of the northern kingdom was so negative that even those who had dedicated their lives to serving God were renouncing their religious vows.

As he preached against the sins of Israel, Amos employed what has been described as the three-fold prophetic task of forthtelling, retelling, and foretelling. In 2:6-8, he addressed the present (forthtelling) by identifying the current sins of Israel. In 2:9-12, Amos recalled the past (retelling) by reminding Israel of God's mighty acts on their behalf: conquests, exodus, guidance through wilderness wandering, the sending of prophets, the calling of Nazirites. Amos concluded his sermon by speaking of the future (foretelling) as he declared God's coming judgment on Israel.

The Coming Judgment of the Lord (2:13-16)

In announcing God's impending judgment, Amos did not use the image of fiery warfare as he did in declaring the Lord's judgment against the previous six nations (1:4, 7, 10, 12, 14; 2:2, 5). The words he employed, however, indicated that the judgment would still be devastating and certain. "I (notice again the divine I) will press you down . . . just as a cart presses down when it is full of sheaves" (2:13), the prophet proclaimed on behalf of God. The image was that of a farmer's cart heavily loaded at harvest time. Such a cart would dig deep ruts into the ground, consequently destroying everything over which it rolled. Just as surely as such an overloaded cart would crush whatever was beneath it, so would God's coming judgment crush Israel.

The verb translated "press down" occurs only here (2:13) in the Old Testament. Difficult to translate, the word may be related to other verbal roots meaning "to split open" or "to tear up." Some scholars have linked this verb with the earthquake mentioned in Amos 1:2 and alluded to

in other passages (3:14ff; 4:11; 6:11; 8:8; 9:1). In conjunction
with the image of the overloaded cart, the probable reference to the earthquake underscored the message of God's
coming judgment on Israel.

Verses 14-16 portray the devastating effects of God's
judgment. The description is of an army in total disarray
after defeat in battle. Not even the swiftest or strongest
Israelites would escape. The bowmen, the foot soldiers, and
the horsemen would lose their lives. Even the most coura-
geous Israelites would flee from the scene in shame.

The Impact of the Sermon

By the conclusion of Amos' sermon, all of the "amen-
preach-on-tell-it-like-it-is" responses had subsided. Amos
had dared to tell it like it was. And it wasn't good! Israel
was saturated with sinners. Israel was about to be judged.

A chilling silence, followed perhaps by disgruntled
mutterings, must have accompanied Amos as he brought
his sermon to a close. No one walked down the aisle during the invitation. No one could really believe that Amos
had spoken the truth. No one shook the preacher's hand
after the service. The Israelite congregation just wanted this
southern preacher from Judah to go back home.

Ah, Israel. Materially rich, yet spiritually poor. So
quick to see the sins of others, so blind to its own mis-
deeds. So caught up in religious privilege, so oblivious to
religious responsibility. So much like so many people
today, so much like so many of us.

Questions for Reflection

1. How did Amos gain the attention of his Israelite audience?

2. What pattern did Amos employ in his sermon (1:3–2:16)?

3. How did Amos demonstrate that God is interested in international politics?

4. List several sins for which Israel was condemned.

Notes

[1]James Limburg, *Hosea-Micah*, "Interpretation: A Biblical Commentary for Teaching and Preaching" (Atlanta: John Knox Press, 1988) 88.

[2]Ralph L. Smith, "Amos," *The Broadman Commentary* (Nashville: Broadman Press, 1972) 91.

[3]Limburg, 88-89.

[4]Ibid.

[5]James Luther Mays, *Amos*, "The Old Testament Library" (Philadelphia: The Westminster Press, 1974) 46.

Chapter 2

Hear This Word Sermonettes against Israel

3:1–6:14

Israel's special calling . . . does not entitle her to
special privilege, but to greater responsibility.
—Bernhard W. Anderson
Understanding the Old Testament

Do you know church members who are quick to claim the
privileges of their faith but who are slow to carry out the
responsibilities that their faith demands? Are you ever one
of these "grace-is-wonderful-but-religious-responsibilities-
are-too-demanding" followers of the faith?

Most of us find it easy and comforting to focus on
the benefits of our belief system: grace, love, peace, forgiveness, eternal life, and so on. Yet, if the truth be known,
most of us find it difficult and even disconcerting to be
reminded of the costs of following God: doing what is right
(justice), treating others with love and kindness, and car-
rying out the responsibilities of our faith in a spirit of
humility.

Throughout his brief but memorable ministry to
Israel, Amos prophesied against folks who were big

proponents of religious pomp and privilege but who were
absentee disciples when it came to living out the demands
of their faith. Indeed, as we have noted, Israel's lack of religious commitment had resulted in a multitude of sins for
which the nation was about to be punished. Amos had the
task of telling Israel that the Lord had finally had enough
of the nation's superficial religion and immoral living. He
proclaimed in superb sermonic fashion,

> Listen up, Israel. The Lord has had it with you.
> Your sins, especially against the "little people" of
> your society, have gone beyond the saturation
> point of God's grace. This whole nation will soon
> reap divine judgment and be destroyed.

Amos delivered this salvo of judgment against Israel
in a masterful sermon (1:3–2:16) that provides the opening
of the book of Amos. In the remaining chapters of the
"words" section of Amos (chapters 3–6), we do not have
another full-length sermon, but rather snippets of sermons
that Amos preached at different times to different Israelite
audiences. These sermonettes provide us with numerous
examples illustrating how eighth-century B.C. Israel was big
on religious privilege but short on faith responsibilities.
        Just because chapters 3–6 contain sermonettes rather
than full-length sermons should not cause us to think that
these sermon briefs were just haphazardly strung together
without forethought or purpose. A close examination of
them reveals the work of Amos' editors (probably his
disciples) who evidently had a plan in mind when they
brought together many of Amos' pronouncements into a
collected whole.

For example, three collections of sermonettes begin with the same phrase: "Hear this" (3:1; 4:1; 5:1; 8:4 in the "visions" section of Amos). In many ways, the sermonettes of Amos in chapters 3–6 provide us with the heart of his message since they often furnish an elaboration of the themes that were mentioned in the unified sermon found in 1:3–2:16.

Listen closely to the sermonettes of Amos. They contain not only God's message for the Israel of Amos'day, but they contain God's timeless message demanding justice and right living on the part of every generation including our own.

Privilege and Responsibility
(Amos 3)

Amos' full-length sermon (1:3–2:16) concluded with the earth-shattering declaration that God would punish the entire nation of Israel because of its sins. This message of divine judgment and destruction must have had a reeling effect on the northern audience. Such a surprisingly harsh doomsday theme would have caused Amos' hearers to pose two major questions: (1) Could this really happen to us, God's chosen people? and (2) With what authority does Amos dare preach to us in this condemnatory way?[1]

The sermonette recorded in verses 1-2 provides an answer to the first question, while verses 3-8, which constitute another sermonette, deal with the second of these questions. Verses 9-15, with which chapter 3 concludes, are oracles or sermon briefs that were apparently grouped together because of their concern with judgment.

Could This Really Happen? (3:1-2)

Both Amos and his northern audience agreed that the people of Israel were God's chosen people. This divine choice could be evidenced in the exodus event by which the Lord rescued the Israelites from Egyptian slavery and in the covenant relationship that God had established with Israel.

Amos referred to the Exodus event when, speaking to Israel for God, he declared: "I brought you up out of the land of Egypt" (v. 1). This often-used phrase was a standardized way to speak of the Exodus (2:10). Amos called attention to God's covenant with Israel through the divine declaration: "You only have I known of all the families of the earth" (v. 2). The word translated "known" in this verse is the Hebrew word *yada'*, a covenant word used to describe a relationship.

Yada' is often used in the Old Testament to refer to the intimate relationship between a husband and wife (Gen 4:1). In other contexts, the word takes on the connotations of to know personally, to love, to elect, to choose (Gen 18:19), and to recognize as a covenant partner. Through his utilization of the word *yada'*, Amos obviously was not saying that Israel was the only nation known by God. As Amos' previous sermon had demonstrated, in a cognitive sense God knew all the nations of the earth (1:3–2:5). In the sense of having a covenant relationship with them, however, God only "knew" one people: Israel.

Amos, then, did not proclaim a new truth by declaring God's election of and covenant with Israel. On the matter of Israel being God's chosen-covenant people, both Amos and his Israelite audience agreed. They differed in their perception of the meaning of being God's chosen people, however.

For Israel, it meant privilege. The Israelites reasoned that since God had chosen them and entered into covenant with them, then the Lord must surely love them more than the other nations. As God's chosen people, Israel expected to receive rich blessings from God. Certainly the political, economic, social, and religious revival under Jeroboam II was an indicator of how privileged and blessed Israel was.

The people eagerly looked forward to the forthcoming "day of the Lord" in which they anticipated a climactic historical occasion when the Lord would further bless the political, economic, social, and religious position of the nation—a day when God would vindicate the Israelites against their enemies and elevate the status of Israel to that of "number one" among the nations of the world (5:18-20). As far as God's judgment was concerned, surely the Lord would be more tolerant and less stringent with Israel.

"Not so!" responded Amos. While acknowledging that election and covenant entailed privilege, Amos insisted that being God's chosen people also called for responsible behavior. Two Old Testament passages are especially helpful in understanding Amos' position. Exodus 19:5 proclaims that God's covenant with Israel rested upon a basic condition: "If you (Israel) obey my voice and keep my covenant, you shall be my [the Lord's] treasured possession out of all the people."

As a representative of this covenant tradition, Amos insisted that Israel had not adhered to God's "if." The nation had not obeyed God's voice and kept the Lord's covenant. Consequently, rather than lessening Israel's punishment, the Lord would heighten the nation's responsibility for its wayward conduct. Not one sin of Israel would escape divine punishment. "Therefore I will punish you for all your iniquities," the Lord told the nation through the preaching of Amos (3:2b).

Genesis 18:19 also illuminates Amos' denunciation of Israel's sins. In this passage, God's special relationship with Abraham—that is, the Lord's choice of Abraham—called for a particular response:

> I have *chosen* [the same Hebrew word translated "known" in Amos 3:2] him, that he may charge his children and his household after him to keep the way of the Lord by doing *righteousness* and *justice*. (author's italics)[2]

This understanding of being "known" and "chosen" by God (represented by the word *yada'*) calls for more than passively receiving divine blessings. God's people (whether Abraham in Genesis 18 or the nation Israel in Amos 3) were known and chosen by God in order to carry out a particular responsibility—namely, to do righteousness and justice. Throughout his preaching ministry to Israel, Amos utilized the same words for righteousness and justice as those employed in Genesis 18:19 (5:24; 5:7; 6:12). In this way, Amos continually reminded his Israelite audience that God desired and expected from the covenant people the practice of righteousness and justice in their daily lives.

"Could the catastrophic judgment of God on Israel as proclaimed by Amos really happen?" the people of Israel asked. "Of course it could, and it will," responded Amos. "Covenant means more than receiving divine blessings and being the recipients of special privileges. Covenant also means responsibility as characterized by the practice of justice and righteousness. This you have failed to do. Therefore, God will punish you for all of your iniquities."

By What Authority Do You Condemn Us? (3:3-8)

Still stunned by Amos' message of judgment and punishment, the Israelites not only wondered: "Could Amos' prophecy really happen?" The northern kingdom audience must have also pondered a second question: "Just who does this southerner Amos think he is anyway? By what authority does he travel up here and condemn us?"

Protests and ridicule based upon this "authority" question evidently greeted Amos whenever and wherever he stopped in Israel to preach. On one such occasion, he skillfully employed rhetoric to answer this authority question by asking his audience seven questions of his own (3:3-6), each of which was designed to elicit a response of "No" from the audience. We can imagine Amos once again using his oratorical prowess to "play" his audience by directly involving them in his address much like he had earlier appealed to the response of his congregation during his initial sermon (1:3–2:16). We can further imagine that Amos, after asking each of the seven questions, paused for effect to allow his words to "sink in" and to evoke—at least silently if not overtly—the response of "No" he desired.

The seven questions deal with the relationship of cause and effect. Like most of his contemporaries, Amos did not believe that any event that occurred was accidental. Ultimately, Amos and his Israelite audience were convinced that every event on earth was the result of God causing or allowing it to happen (3:6b) The relationship between the events and their respective causes that are contained in Amos' seven questions can be listed according to the following chart.

Verse	Event	Cause
3	two people walking together	they had made an appointment to do so
4a	a lion roars in the forest	the lion has captured some prey
4b	a young lion cries out from its den	the lion has caught something
5a	a bird falls on the ground	a net or trap has ensnared it
5b	a trap springs shut	something has touched the trigger
6a	the people in a city are afraid	the trumpet (alarm) in the city has sounded signaling an enemy's approach
6b	a city experiences disaster	the Lord has caused it

In masterful sermonic fashion, Amos formulated each of these cause and effect relationships into a question to which his audience's response was most certainly "No." Then having immersed his audience in the "cause and effect" way of thinking, Amos brought his sermonette to a climax by asking two additional "cause and effect" type questions (v. 8). First he asked: "The lion has roared (cause); who will not fear (event)?" The obvious answer from the audience was "No one!" Secondly he posited this inquiry: "The Lord has spoken (cause); who can but prophesy (event)?" The response from the audience could only be "No one!"

Through this series of questions dealing with cause and effect, in essence Amos was saying:

> The *event* of my preaching to you is *caused* by God having told me to preach. Just as two people walk together (event) because they previously made an appointment (cause); just as a lion roars (event) because he has captured his prey (cause); just as a bird falls to the ground (event) because it has been ensnared by a net (cause); just as a city becomes frightened (event) because the alarm signaling an approaching enemy has been sounded (cause); just as people become afraid (event) because a lion has roared (cause); . . . so do I prophesy and preach to you a message of judgment (event) because God has spoken and commanded me to do so (cause)!

With ingenious homiletical skill, Amos provided the answer to the "by-what-authority-do-you-condemn-us?" concern of the Israelites. "By God's authority" was the prophet's reply. It was a matter of divine cause and effect. Amos had been given the word of the Lord, and he *had* to proclaim it!

Note that verse 7 breaks the flow of rhetorical questions. For this reason, some scholars view this verse as a later editorial insertion. Whether an original part of the sermonette or a commentary added by one of Amos' later disciples, the verse declares something significant about the nature of Israel's God. The Lord would not capriciously send divine judgment on a people without first issuing a warning to those people via the prophets.

At times the warning offered a chance for the people to repent and consequently delay God's judgment or even make it unnecessary. At other times, however, the warning declared God's certain impending judgment because the sins of a people had exceeded a "saturation point" beyond which the Lord would not allow matters to continue without some type of punishment.

In its own way, verse 7 also justifies Amos' message of judgment to Israel. Through the prophet Amos, God revealed the divine plan to judge Israel (whose sins according to Amos 2:6 had exceeded the "for-three-transgressions-and-for-four" saturation point) several years prior to the time when the nation in 722 B.C. was ultimately judged.

In summary, the first two sermonettes in chapter 3 were employed by Amos to provide a defense of his message and ministry. Although the Israelites were God's chosen-covenant people, the northern kingdom would still reap God's judgment because being God's chosen people entailed not only privileges received but responsible living practiced (3:1-2). And although the doom and gloom message that Amos preached against Israel was unpopular if not dangerous, Amos still had to preach it because he was authorized and called by God to do so. Amos could not bring himself to do otherwise (3:3-8).

Sermonettes of Judgment (3:9-15)

Chapter three concludes with a grouping of sermonettes that share the common theme of judgment. As these oracles demonstrate, Amos was not content to give a blanket condemnation against the sins of the whole nation of Israel in _general_. The prophet felt compelled to become more focused in his proclamation of doom by targeting more specific audiences within the northern kingdom.

Judgment on Samaria (3:9-12). We can reasonably assume that Amos was in Samaria, the capital city of the northern kingdom, when this sermonette was delivered. We can also deduce that his target audience was the members of the royal and upper classes who lived, ruled, reigned, and conducted business in the capital city. As we might expect from what we already know about Amos, his message to these powerful Israelite politicians, governmental bureaucrats, and wealthy business people would not be of the "God-bless-you-what-wonderful followers-of-the-Lord-you-are" variety. True to his calling, Amos was about to unleash another doom-and-gloom tirade.

But how could he gain and hold his audience's attention? After all, word was starting to spread about this fiery preacher from the south, and Amos knew that even the most receptive audience (which Israel certainly was not) would "tune out" a speaker if presentations were always basically the same.

Ever creative in his preaching, Amos secured the attention of his Samaria audience by employing drama, imagination, and irony. Specifically, he pretended to issue a summons to heralds, authorizing them to carry an invitation to the ruling and upper level business classes of Ashdod (Philistia) and Egypt. That Amos was inviting representatives from these elite and powerful classes of Ashdodites and Egyptians is indicated by his use of the word "strongholds" (3:9-10), which refers to the multi-storied buildings where the royal and upper echelon people of class-structured societies worked and lived. This imaginary invitation was for representatives of Ashdod's and Egypt's "strongholds" to visit Samaria.

What would representatives of these pagan governments find if such a visit to Samaria were to take place? They would witness "great tumults" and "oppressions" (3:9). "Tumults" is the translation for a Hebrew word often rendered as "confusion" or "panic." The Hebrew word translated "oppressions" (also used in 4:1) refers to the oppression of the less fortunate by the wealthy. Amos' implication was both ironic and clear. Even representatives from Ashdod and Egypt where the Lord was not worshiped would be astounded by the degree of sin and oppression in Samaria!

With his audience attentive to his preaching, Amos issued perhaps the most incriminating denunciation of all: the inhabitants of Samaria "do not know how to do right" (3:10). So superficial had been their religion, so secure had become their materialistic lifestyle, and so sinful had become their oppressive actions, that they had become desensitized and numb to the way that God's chosen people should live. Like all of the inhabitants throughout the northern kingdom, the Israelites in Samaria still viewed being the chosen people of God as a privilege to be enjoyed rather than as a responsibility to be lived.

The inevitable result? God's punishment and judgment. Still holding the attention of his capital city congregation, Amos proclaimed and described God's coming judgment as a successful military campaign against Samaria. Although he did not identify the particular military foe, the internationally and politically astute Amos undoubtedly had Assyria in mind. All too soon, prophetic pronouncement would become historical reality. The city of Samaria was overthrown by the Assyrians in 722 B.C.

This particular sermonette against Samaria concludes with a proverb (3:12) that is drawn from the tradition of wisdom literature. Amos was evidently quite familiar with both the content and style of the wisdom school of his day (1:3 and the other references to "for three transgressions of ___ and for four; 3:3-6). He compared the fate of Samaria/Israel with the remains of a sheep that had been devoured by a lion. Shepherds in Amos' day were required to produce evidence for the sheep owner that the loss of a sheep or lamb was the result of an attack by a predatory animal. The required evidence was the remains of the dead carcass (Exod 22:10-13; Gen 31:39).

Amos' use of this proverb, then, in no way suggested that a remnant of Samaria/Israel would survive the coming divine judgment. On the contrary, the use of this particular proverb declared that the only rescue that the Israelites in Samaria could expect would be like the shepherd's rescue of a dead sheep's remains in order to prove that the sheep has been killed. Following the coming judgment, only broken pieces of Samaria's opulent lifestyle—"the corner of a couch and part of a bed"—would remain. For Amos, God's impending punishment of Samaria would be absolutely complete and certain.

Judgment on Bethel (3:13-14). The religious capital of the northern kingdom was Bethel, located approximately ten miles north of Jerusalem. Also known as the royal sanctuary, Bethel would be the site of Amos' well-known confrontation with Amaziah the priest who was on the royal payroll of King Jeroboam II (7:10-17). Other sermonettes by Amos (4:4; 5:5) would also mention Bethel in a judgmental manner because Israelite worship at Bethel, while liturgically correct, had no impact on the daily living and ethical conduct of the worshipers.

In this brief oracle, the ever versatile preacher Amos employed the imagery of the courtroom to "call" imaginary witnesses to testify against Israel (3:13). Essentially, Amos portrayed the Lord as taking Israel to court because of the nation's multitudinous transgressions. And the verdict of this divine courtroom? "Guilty," God through the prophet declared. And the subsequent sentence? "The downfall and destruction of the nation, even the national religious headquarters at Bethel," the Lord through Amos proclaimed (3:14).

The "horns of the altar" mentioned in 3:14 were little pillars or symbolic figures on the corners of the altar that somewhat resembled the horns of an ox. A person could find a place of refuge from his enemies by entering the temple and actually grasping these "horns" (1 Kgs 1:50; 2:28). To underscore how thorough God's judgment against Bethel and Israel would be, Amos pictured a scenario wherein the horns of the altar at Bethel would be cut off and cast down. Even Israel's last resort of security—the horns of the altar in the sanctuary at the nation's religious capital—would be destroyed. Even Bethel (which means "house of God") would not escape the coming judgment of the Lord against Israel.

Judgment on the status symbols of the "new rich" (3:15). One of the signs of wealth in eighth-century B.C. Israel was evidently the ownership of more than one home. Apparently, some of Israel's well-to-do citizens had both winter and summer houses. The use of ivory in the construction of such homes is a further indicator that Israel's upper class had luxurious lifestyles and lavish tastes. Amos had a problem with this situation in that these wealthy Israelites, especially the rapidly growing "new-rich," often amassed their fortunes and impressive financial portfolios at the expense of the poor (2:6-8). Such unjust and selfish action could not escape divine detection and condemnation. Just as Israel's transgressions would result in the downfall of the "house of God" (Beth-El), so would the wrongs of Israel's new wealthy class ultimately result in the destruction of the houses of people.

Despite the unpopularity of his "doom and gloom" preaching, Amos did not back off from proclaiming God's judgment. Whether he found himself in the political capital (Samaria), in the midst of the nation's religious headquarters (Bethel), or in the presence of Israel's rapidly emerging upper class, Amos dared to deliver his "Thus says the Lord" messages of divine destruction that would soon befall the nation.

Wicked Women
Hypocritical Worship
Ignored Warnings
(Amos 4)

The sermonettes of Amos that are recorded in chapter 4 underscore the tenacity and resolve (his hearers would call it stubbornness) with which the prophet proclaimed God's message of judgment to various groups of Israelites. Amos backed down from no one, as his condemnatory messages in this chapter suggest.

"Cows of Bashan": The Women of Samaria (4:1-3)

Amos did not confine his preaching to the male segment of Israel's population. He dared to condemn the Israelite women for their sins, too, and he did so in a rather shocking manner.

We can imagine Amos strolling into the market place of Samaria where many of the well-to-do Israelite ladies regularly gathered for shopping and conversation. After observing them for a while, Amos felt it was time for a "hear this word" message. His voice startled the women, but not nearly as much as the manner in which Amos addressed them. "Here this word, you cows of Bashan who are on Mount Samaria," he proclaimed.

The territory of Bashan was located in Transjordan, east of the Sea of Galilee. It was a region noted for rich, lush pasture lands (Jer 50:19; Micah 7:14) and particularly for fine cattle (Deut 32:14; Ezek 39:18; Ps 22:12). As Amos reflected on the lifestyles of the wealthy women of Samaria, the image of the sleek, fat, contented Bashan cattle emerged in his mind.

Some scholars have argued that calling these women "cows of Bashan" was not necessarily derogatory. In the Song of Solomon (4:1-4), for example, a young lover speaks of the beauty of his beloved by comparing her teeth to a flock of shorn ewes and her hair to a flock of goats! But this was poetic language used in a love poem designed for a woman whom the author knew personally and well. Even this "head-over-heels-in-love" poet did not actually call his lover a ewe or a goat. He knew better! Granted, the Bashan cattle were widely recognized for being well-bred, well-groomed, superb quality cattle. But that did not mean that a woman would consider it a compliment to be called a Bashan cow, especially by some strange out-of-town shepherd from Judah as he stood in the public arena of the marketplace preaching against a number of the leading women in the city.

No, Amos was not handing out compliments when he addressed those Israelite women in the capital city of Samaria as "cows of Bashan." He was gaining the attention of his audience. Once he got their attention (and it did not take long), Amos really let them have it:

> You cows of Bashan. Hear this word of the Lord. You are as guilty before God as your politician and businessmen husbands. In fact, you urge and persuade your husbands to maintain your extravagant and luxurious lifestyles. Your spouses increase their incomes and support your lavish tastes at the expense of the poor whom they overcharge and cheat. While you live a spoiled, pampered existence, the less fortunate in your society struggle to make ends meet. In your own way—as you sit back and drink your expensive wine and indulge in other extravagant tastes—you also oppress the poor and crush the needy. You, too, will be punished and judged by the Lord.

The impact of Amos' sermonette against the women of Samaria was similar to that of a visiting evangelist coming to a church field for a revival and taking on the women's missionary group (or at least the local woman's club)! But Amos backed down to no one, not even the leading women of the town and church. His scathing verbal attack against the women of Samaria was somewhat like the critical words that Isaiah, a contemporary of Amos,

proclaimed against the women of Jerusalem (Isa 3:16–4:1).
If the women were shocked (as they most certainly must
have been), Amos was not deterred. He moved directly
from identifying the sins of the women (v. 1) to announcing what the Lord's judgment against the ladies in Samaria
would be (vv. 2-3).

The certainty of coming judgment is emphasized in
the phrase "The Lord God has sworn by his holiness" (v.
2). The holiness of God is the divine otherness of God—the
dynamic that separates the Lord from everything else. For
God, then, to swear "by his holiness" essentially means that
God swears by God's self. The Lord had taken an oath that
coming judgment upon the "cows of Bashan"/women of
Samaria would be sure!

What would be the nature of this divine punishment? The women would be taken away with "hooks" and
"fishooks" (v. 2). The Hebrew words translated "hooks"
and "fishooks" in verse 2 occur no other place in the Old
Testament with this meaning. Consequently, the precise
fate of the women is open to interpretation. Hooks could be
used to drag away corpses or to join together prisoners
who would be led away into exile. Whether "flung out" (v.
3) of the city as corpses or as prisoners marching into exile,
the fate of the Israelite females would be horrible.

In further elaborating upon the judgment that
would befall Samaria's women, verse 3 can be interpreted
as continuing with the bovine "women-as-cows" imagery.
The women are portrayed as being prodded and forced out
of the city through breaches in the city walls much like cattle would be driven through holes in a fence. Harmon
(4:3b), the destination of the exiled women, has not been
identified geographically and is often amended to read
"Herman." As a geographical site, Herman was located in

the region of Bashan. How ironic that the women whom Amos called "cows of Bashan" were being exiled to Bashan! How further ironic that the "cows of Bashan" who treated the poor of Israel like cattle were being treated like cattle themselves!

Interestingly, Amos indicted both the men and women of the northern kingdom for sins against the poor and defenseless ones in society. The specific indictment against the men for abusing and mistreating the poor is contained in Amos 8:4-8. According to this passage, the men actually committed the specific sins against the less fortunate by overcharging them for merchandise, employing other unethical business practices, and even selling them as slaves.

While the women apparently did not directly engage in such wrongful actions, they encouraged their husbands to commit such wrongs so that more wealth could be attained to insure the continuance of their luxurious and extravagant lifestyles. For Amos, the women were just as responsible for these crimes against the poor as their husbands. Thus did Amos dare to preach against and pronounce divine judgment upon the spoiled, wealthy Israelite women in Samaria—the "cows of Bashan."

Sinful, Self-serving Worship (4:4-5)

We have already identified Bethel as the religious headquarters of the northern kingdom and the site of the royal sanctuary supported by King Jeroboam II. Gilgal, also mentioned in this sermonette (4:4), was the second leading religious center in Israel during the time of Amos. Just the mention of these two cities in the first part of this brief oracle alerts us to the great probability that Amos will preach about religion. From what we already know about this fiery orator, the slant of the sermonette will not be positive.

Amos does not disappoint us. The brief sermonette in verses 4-5 takes on a negative judgmental tone. The highly imaginative and ever creative Amos once again surprises us with his presentation. His original hearers—probably those assembling at Bethel and Gilgal—were no doubt surprised as well.

The worshipers at the Israelite sanctuaries were accustomed to having a priest greet them with a call to worship such as: "O come, let us worship and bow down; let us kneel before the Lord, our Maker!" (Ps 95:6) Consequently, to hear Amos outside their sanctuary reciting a call to worship was not all that unusual. Perhaps they initially thought that Amos was a guest priest, just "filling the pulpit" for their regular minister. Why, the Israelites were so familiar with the words of those calls to worship that they could tell you what would be said without giving it a second thought!

"Come to Bethel and worship; come to Gilgal and bow down before the Lord." "Same old stuff," they reasoned as they almost mindlessly started to mouth the words along with the guest speaker when it suddenly became apparent that something was different. The guest minister was changing the call to worship, and it was not a change for the good!

"Come to Bethel—and transgress; to Gilgal—and multiply transgression." With skillful and sharp satire, Amos attacked the worship of the Israelites. The word "transgression" often has the connotation of rebellion, especially the rebellion of a grown child against loving parents (Isa 1:2; Prov 28:24). "Come to worship and rebel against the Lord," Amos was saying. "Come to church services and sin!"

Why this satirical sermonette condemning Israel's worship? Later, Amos condemned Israel's worship because it had no impact upon how the people conducted themselves when they were not in church (5:21-24). In this sermonette, however, he condemned the worship because rather than focusing attention upon God, it focused attention upon the people. Notice the emphasis with which Amos spoke of "your sacrifices" and "your tithes" (v. 4). Amos' command to "proclaim freewill offerings" and "publish them" (v. 5) further demonstrates the desire of the worshipers to be publicly recognized for their worship and generosity.

Amos concluded this surprising call to worship by telling why the people attended worship. In a traditional call to worship, this concluding segment would declare something like: "For the Lord is our God and we are his people" (Ps 95:6-7). Amos' satirical version concluded by saying, "for so you love to do, O people of Israel" (v. 5).

It was not for God's sake that the people of the northern kingdom flocked to Bethel and Gilgal. It was for their own sakes and the enhancement of their own reputations that they worshiped regularly at the nation's leading religious sanctuaries. Such self-serving religion was sinful according to Amos. Pleasing to God it was not.

Amos' hearers were less than thrilled when they realized the motive behind the prophet's satirical sermonizing. How dare Amos accuse them of hypocritical religious practices! (How did the prophet "see through" our well-performed religious practices?) Perhaps a loose contemporary paraphrase of Amos 4:4-5 will help us grasp the feelings and reactions of Amos'audience:

Come to Nashville—and transgress; to Atlanta—
and multiply transgression. Bring *your* best
preachers and soloists, *your* most accomplished
choirs and drama troupes. Bring *your* tithes and
money—*your* contributions to the foreign, home,
and state mission offerings. Proclaim *your* annual
church report and the record of *your* vital sta-
tistics (the number of baptisms, *your* average
Sunday School attendance, and the amount of
your annual budget). Be sure to publish them; for
so you love to do, O people. For so you love to
do.

Rejected Warnings and Missed Chances (4:6-12)

Some hearers of Amos' doomsday preaching might have
assumed that the prophet portrayed God as some type of
"unmerciful-legalistic-mess-up-once-and-you've-had-it"
deity whose favorite pastime consisted of capriciously pun-
ishing the people for the smallest transgression or sin. "Not
so!" Amos essentially declared in this poetic sermonette.
The response of Amos to this totally false assumption
would have been something like the following:

Not so! In fact, just the opposite is true. God
doesn't desire to punish Israel. Yet, Israel has left
God no other option. Time and time again, the
Lord has warned the Israelites of their sins and
called upon them to repent. Yet, the people have
ignored God's warnings. They have not repented
and returned to God. They continuously have
duped themselves into believing that God will

not punish them because they are God's chosen
people.

Well, the Lord has had enough. Since
Israel has not responded to the Lord's warnings,
the nation will certainly receive God's judgment.
Israel had better prepare to meet God in a way
it has not previously anticipated because judgment in the form of destruction is about to occur!

For Amos, God had sent warnings to Israel in the
form of a series of calamities that had been intended to
cause the people to repent and return to God. Specifically,
Amos enumerated seven such calamity-warnings: famine
(cleanness of teeth and lack of bread, v. 6), drought (v. 7),
blight of mildew that caused crop failure (v. 9a), locusts (v.
9b), pestilence (v. 10a), war (v. 10b), and earthquake (v. 11).

Once again demonstrating his preaching creativity
and oratorical skills, Amos interspersed this catalogue of
calamity with the recurring phrase "yet you did not return
to me, says the Lord" (verses 6, 8, 9, 10, 11). This phrase
serves as a thematic refrain that throughout the sermonette
echoes the sad but all-too-true fact that Israel has repeatedly ignored the warnings of God. Even after the sermonette
was over, this refrain must have continued to reverberate
in the ears and minds of Amos' audience.

All seven calamities mentioned in verses 6-11 occurred periodically in eighth-century B.C. Israel. Amos
seemed to indicate that all seven of these warnings had
been experienced by the Israelites of his day—not all at
once, of course, but over a period of several years. Some of
these calamities may have been experienced by previous
generations of Israelites and kept alive through the col-
lective memory of succeeding generations. Perhaps these

seven calamities were part of the "curses" in the "blessings
and curses" portion of an annual covenant renewal ceremony—curses that the Lord would send against Israel if
the people did not live according to the terms of their covenant with God (Lev 26; Deut 28).

Whether occurring in the present or in the past or
emphasized in the context of a covenant renewal ceremony,
the seven calamities mentioned by Amos were enumerated
for the purpose of demonstrating that Israel had ignored
God's warnings. The Lord, via these calamities, had given
Israel all sorts of chances to repent. That there were seven
calamities may very well be significant. God's offer of
chances for Israel to repent and return was complete. Yet,
Israel refused. The people's sins exceeded the "saturation
point" beyond which God would not allow their sins to go
unpunished (2:6-8). Judgment was inevitable.

Whenever a verse in Amos begins with "therefore,"
the reader/hearer should be alert to an announcement
about judgment. With its "therefore" beginning, verse 12
announces God's judgment upon Israel. The judgment announcement is very vague: "Thus will I do to you, O Israel
. . . prepare to meet your God." Amos did not specify what
God would do as judgment upon Israel. This contrasts with
most other occasions when Amos was quite specific in his
declaration of divine judgment (1:3–2:16; 3:11).

Such vagueness has caused some scholars to specu-
late that a more precise description of judgment was an
original part of this passage—a specific judgment description that somehow dropped out of this text somewhere
along the way of the editorial/transmission process. Still
others have stated that having to meet God, after having
repeatedly ignored the warnings of God, is "definite
enough" in terms describing God's coming judgment.

"Prepare to meet your God" in verse 12b is not one final appeal for the people to repent and avoid divine judgment. The appeals process had been exhausted. The offer of warnings was complete. The saturation point of Israel's sins had been exceeded. "Prepare to meet your God" was Amos' way of emphasizing that divine judgment would unquestionably fall upon the northern kingdom. Or as Amos would later express the matter,

> Why do you want the day of the Lord? It is darkness not light. . . . Is not the day of the Lord darkness . . . and gloom with no brightness in it? (5:18, 20)

A Doxology (4:13)

Chapter 4 concludes with the first of three doxologies found in Amos (4:13; 5:8-9; 9:5-6). In these doxologies, the Lord is praised as the God of creation. The awesome power of the Creator is affirmed. Originally, all three of these doxologies may well have been part of a single hymn of praise that was known by Amos and/or his disciples. All three of these doxological hymn fragments end with the phrase "the Lord is his name" (4:13; 5:9; 9:6).

As a shepherd-farmer, Amos would have been quite familiar with the power and majesty of God that is manifested in nature. Such a powerful deity was certainly more than capable of bringing about the punishment that would fall on Israel. This is the God whom Israel would meet in judgment.

Death and Deportation: the Results of Injustice
(Amos 5)

Chapter 5 begins with another "hear this word" pronouncement that serves as an introduction for another grouping of
Amos' sermonettes (3:1; 4:1; 8:4). The sermonettes recorded
in this chapter represent some of the most significant oracles that Amos delivered. In a sense, chapter 5 really
contains the heart of the book of Amos. In it Amos' major
themes of justice and righteousness, which are hinted at
and implicitly referred to in earlier chapters, are explicitly
mentioned. Indeed, here we find the great summary verse
of Amos: "But let justice roll down like waters and righteousness like an ever-flowing stream" (5:24).

By the end of chapter 5, there is no question as to
what God demanded of Israel: justice and righteousness.
Also by the conclusion of this chapter, there is no question
why Israel would be punished via exile: the practice of justice and righteousness the nation had forsaken.

A Funeral for Israel (5:1-3)

How would you react if your minister stepped into the pulpit this coming Sunday morning and said, "We gather
today for the funeral of our church"? In essence, that is
what Amos said in verses 1-3. Once again exhibiting his
preaching versatility, Amos couched his message in the
form of a funeral dirge. He sang a mourning song for the
nation: "Fallen, no more to rise, is the virgin Israel" (v. 2).

Throughout his other messages, Amos spoke God's
coming judgment against Israel. In these verses, however,

Amos treats Israel's fall as something that had already happened. The "death" had occurred so the funeral song was sung. So certain was Amos of God's judgment against Israel that he spoke/sang of it as a past event.

The Hebrew word for lamentation in verse 1 is *qinah*, the word used to describe a composition to be sung by professional mourners who played an accepted and important role in Old Testament society (Jer 9:17, 20; Ezek 32:16; 2 Chron 35:25). These professional mourners assisted grieving persons by encouraging them to seek and express their emotions. Some scholars have even suggested that Amos clothed himself in the attire of a professional mourner before delivering this funeral song sermonette. This might have been the first dramatic monologue sermonette on record!

Whether or not Amos "dressed up" for this part, the meter and form of the *qinah* were so well known that his audience would have almost immediately understood the message. They did not have to be told that he was speaking to them as he vocalized this dirge.

The mourning song portrays Israel as a virgin, a young woman whose life is ravaged by an invading army. There is no one to rescue her or "to raise her up" (v. 2). Her premature demise denies her the opportunities of fulfilling her potential as a wife, mother, and adult. Like the fallen virgin, the nation Israel had "died" before her time. While singing the mourning song to convey God's message of judgment, Amos himself may well have been mourning as he reflected on the tremendous opportunities that Israel —because of its sins of injustice—had wasted.

Verse 3 describes the catastrophe that caused Israel's fall, necessitating the singing of the dirge in verse 2. The scene describes a highly effective military campaign against

Israel. In an attempt to counter the invasion by the uniden-
tified enemy force, the cities of Israel are pictured as sending out their armed forces for battle. However, the results
for Israel were disastrous.

Only 10 percent of each city's military forces
returned. The returning 10 percent should not be viewed as
some type of remnant that would survive Israel's fall.
Amos emphasized the 90 percent who were destroyed. The
small portion that managed to return symbolized defeat in
much the same manner that the remnant of a sheep that
has been devoured by a lion symbolized complete destruction (see comments on 3:12). Verse 3 is a portrait signifying
destruction and not hope. Remember, the song that Amos
was called to sing was not a grace note but a dirge.

A Prescription for Life (5:4-7)

From singing a funeral dirge of death, Amos moved to
teaching a lesson about life. To accomplish this, he assumed
the role of a priest giving instruction or torah to his parishioners. Hearing the command "to seek the Lord" was a
fairly common occurrence for religious folks of Old Testament times (Deut 4:29; Jer 29:13; Isa 55:6-7; Ps 27:8; 24:6;
105:4). In fact, upon hearing Amos declare "Seek the Lord
and live" (vv. 4, 6), the Israelites probably responded: "No
problem. We're already doing that, Amos. We're seeking
God by going to the sanctuaries regularly for services and
sacrifices. Move on to your next point, Amos. We are
already seeking the Lord by religiously going to church!"

Amos had previously indicted Israel for sinning
rather than worshiping God at Bethel and Gilgal because
the religious activities conducted there focused attention
and acclaim upon the people instead of on the worship of

God (4:4-5). At this juncture, Amos continued to astound his church-going hearers by once again turning their comfortable religious system upside down:

> Seek God and you will live—that's right. But you don't know what seeking God really means. You act as if it only entails attending services at First Church Bethel or Second Church Gilgal with a religious retreat down south to Beersheba thrown in every now and then for good measure. You're wrong. Seeking the Lord means obeying the Lord's commandments. It means practicing justice and righteousness in your daily life. Yet, that's not happening in the lives of you Israelites who substitute church membership and attendance for right living.
>
> You won't even find the Lord at your sanctuaries and religious gatherings. The services and assemblies there have become ends in themselves. It's no sense seeking God where external religious ritual is king and where justice and righteousness are absent. Besides, Bethel and Gilgal are going to be judged and condemned.

For Amos, the prescription for life was not to be found in external religion that was void of responsible, righteous behavior. Real life had its source in God. Communion with God did not result in some type of superficial religiosity or "Sunday only" commitment. Rather, communion with this life-giving Lord resulted in a covenant relationship with God and others—a covenant communion characterized by justice and righteousness.

Verse 7 marks the first time that Amos actually used the words "justice" and "righteousness," although the concepts behind these terms permeate all of the prophet's preaching and ministry. The Hebrew term translated justice is *mishpat*, while the Hebrew word rendered righteousness is *tsedaqah*. On three occasions in Amos, these two terms appear together (5:7; 5:24; 6:12b). On one occasion, justice (*mishpat*) appears alone (5:15).

In the book of Amos, justice has a judicial flavor and refers to doing what is right in the law courts. As we will discover, "court" in Amos' day was held in the city gate (5:10, 12, 15). Such proceedings administered in the gate were not always just. Bribery was rampant, the poor were often treated unfairly, and the integrity of the court system was highly questionable because justice was not practiced—that is, in the area of law and justice, the "in charge" and "money" people would not do what was right.

Closely associated with the judicial term of justice is the relational concept of righteousness. For Amos, righteousness involved having and maintaining appropriate relationships to God and other people based on the terms of a covenant. Justice and righteousness, then, are very closely related. Indeed, possessing righteousness results in the practice of doing what is right—of practicing justice—in one's relationships with both God and others. Justice can be perceived as the fruit or result of righteousness.

Sadly, both justice and righteousness were in short supply among the Israelites of the eighth century B.C. Indeed, Amos declared that the people of Israel had turned "justice to wormwood" and cast "righteousness to the ground." Wormwood was a plant found in Israel that had an extremely bitter taste and whose juice could be poisonous. In the Old Testament, it was used metaphorically to describe something that was distasteful and even toxic (Amos 6:12; Jer 9:15; 23:15; Lam 3:15, 19).

There was no "sweet justice" in the court system of the northern kingdom, only bitter bribery and continuous corruption. The situation with righteousness was not any better. Instead of upholding righteousness—that is, appropriate relationships with God and others—as a standard to be emulated, the more well-to-do "in charge" Israelites were in effect trampling righteousness into the ground. Through the corrupt unjust judicial system as well as through other unfair business transactions, the "poor" and other "little people" of Israelite society were being trampled into "the dust of the earth" (2:7).

Amos really did desire that the Israelites "seek the Lord," but the prophet knew that the sanctuaries of Gilgal and Bethel (much less the court system in the city gate) were not where God was to be found. Right relationships with God and others (righteousness) were not the focus of the sanctuaries. Doing what was right outside the church building when church was not in session (justice) was not emphasized in the worship services. The sanctuaries had become places where the people could go through the motions, pay their religious dues, and call attention to themselves. Void of justice and righteousness and God, the worship centers of Israel had become ends in themselves. Indeed, they were about to end!

Did Amos hold out any hope for the northern kingdom? The phrase "seek the Lord and live *or* he will break out against [Israel] . . . and devour Bethel" seems to hint at the possibility of hope if Israel would repent and seek the Lord via the routes of righteousness and justice. Other glimmers of hope occasionally surfaced in the midst of the prophet's "doom and gloom" preaching (5:14-15; 9:8; 9:11-15). Such faint flickerings of hope should not be perceived as precluding the coming judgment that the Lord pronounced on Israel. Sure Amos wanted Israel to seek God and get straightened out! Yet, as much as he hoped that this might happen, he knew in his heart that such a turnaround would not occur.

The sins of the people had exceeded the "saturation point" beyond which divine judgment was inevitable (2:6-7). The Lord's judgment had been pronounced. The funeral song had been sung. Any hope for the nation would occur on the other side of the coming destruction and fall. With this type of post-judgment hope, the book of Amos concludes (9:11-15).

Another Doxology (5:8-9)

Verses 8-9 constitute the second of three doxologies that appear in Amos (4:13; 9:5-6). All three praise God as the Lord of creation. Originally these doxologies may have come from a single hymn that was known and used by Amos or his disciples. This particular doxology praises God as the creator of the Pleiades and Orion, two prominent and well-known constellations in Old Testament times (Job 9:9; 38:31). Since some ancient peoples worshiped the stars and constellations as gods, Amos' utilization of this doxology that affirms the Lord as the creator of these constellations underscores the power of the Lord as the creator of the universe.

The Lord's power is also highlighted in the second half of this doxology. Through the imagery of war, God is portrayed as being more powerful than even the strongest armies and most fortified defenses. Perhaps the purpose of the hymn was to remind Amos' hearers that the Lord whom they were to seek was a universal, powerful deity with more than enough power to enact judgment against the unjust and unrighteous citizens of Israel.

In the Gate (5:10-13)

"In the gate" refers to the location in each Israelite city where the people of that city assembled to hold court and dispense justice. The city gate was actually a rather large multi-chambered fortification that was built into the city wall. Besides protecting the entrance to the city, the gate area also provided the people with a place to gather and mingle. So it was within this gathering and mingling area of the city gate that the Israelites assembled for court (Ruth 4:1-11; Deut 22:15; 25:7; Job 5:4; 31:21).

The phrase "in the gate" is used three times in chapter five (5:10, 12, 15). We can imagine Amos actually standing in the gate area of a major city (probably Bethel or Gilgal) when he declared that what Israel was dispensing through the court in the gate was certainly not justice. Recall how Amos had previously declared that justice had turned to wormwood—that is, injustice had replaced justice as the order of the day (5:7).

In this passage Amos proclaims that matters have declined to such an extent that anyone who attempts to "reprove" or rebuke the wrong within the judicial system is hated. Persons who dared to speak the truth in court were detested (5:10). The "one who reproves in the gate" is a reference to the elder or foreman of an Israelite jury whose responsibility was to announce the jury's verdict (Prov 24:23-25; Isa 29:29). The "one who speaks the truth" describes a truthful witness testifying before the court. Israel's court system was so corrupt that responsible jurors who attempted to do what was right and honest witnesses who sought to tell the truth were abhorred by the "establishment" of Israelite society.

Why was a just and ethical court system missing and not even desired in the northern kingdom? Perhaps a corrupt court system contributed to the crimes of the rich against the poor—crimes such as those mentioned by Amos in verse 11. The "criminals" were the wealthy landowners who overcharged their tenant farmers by taking more than their rightful share of the crops. When such victimized tenants took their complaints to the court in the gate, they found no advocates nor justice. The court system was rigged in favor of the rich.

Bribes were taken, and the needy element of society such as poor tenant farmers were in essence "pushed aside" (v. 12). The refusal and/or inability to come up with enough money for a bribe meant that many poorer Israelites could not even get their complaints before the court. They found it difficult to have their case put on the docket.

Fearing no recrimination from the court system, the powerful and rich Israelites continued to cheat and exploit the Israelite poor, becoming wealthier in the process. Crime did pay in Israel. The corrupt court system assured that it did. Yet, the days of "crime does pay" and "the court system being corrupt" were numbered, according to Amos. So imminent was God's coming judgment that the Israelites who built new fancy homes and planted picturesque vineyards with the financial gain derived from exploiting the poor would not be able to enjoy them (v. 11). So devastating would be this divine judgment that the only response would be stunned silence (v. 13).

A Second Prescription for Life (5:14-15)

Amos once again assumed the role of a priest giving instruction or teaching torah to his parishioners (5:4-6). Previously, Amos took on this priestly role in order to refute the commonly held belief that the way to seek God was by going regularly to the religious sanctuaries for worship services. "Not necessarily so," Amos had declared. "Seeking God means more than going to church; it means living by God's principles when church is not in session" (5:4-7). In the second priestly discourse, Amos instructed the Israelites to "seek good and not evil" if they really desired the Lord to be with them (v. 14). The "good" is defined as establishing "justice in the gate" (v. 15). In essence, Amos was saying:

> If you are serious about seeking God and being God's people, then act like it. God's presence with you is not automatic and condition free. It depends upon your willingness to practice justice in the gate—to do what is right in the court system and in all areas of public and private life. Seeking good—doing what is right and just— should be the result of your relationship with God. Seeking and responding to God should make a difference in how you live.

Most persons who heard Amos disagreed, however. They believed that God would be with them "regardless"! They were so caught up in the privileges of being the Lord's chosen people that they had all but forgotten or at least conveniently ignored the responsibilities. The "good" was not sought. Justice in the gate (or anywhere else for that matter) was not established. Amos' message of God's imminent judgment against the nation was not really heard.

The last part of this brief sermonette can be construed as containing a note of hope for the "remnant of Joseph" (v. 15b). "Joseph" is sometimes used to refer to the entire northern kingdom since the so-called Joseph tribes, Ephraim and Manasseh, were the two major Israelite tribes in the north (5:6; 6:6). Notice that the hope for God's graciousness was for the "remnant of Joseph"—that is, for those Israelites who would be left after God's devastating judgment on the nation. In no way does verse 15b preclude or even postpone the punishment that God was about to send against Israel. In fact, the concept of a remnant infers that a destructive judgment would occur after which some survivors would remain. Amos held open the possibility that after the coming judgment God "may be" gracious to and even begin again with a remnant of Joseph.

Your Future is a Funeral (5:16-17)

Chapter 5 begins with Amos singing a funeral dirge for Israel (5:1-3) and then moves to the prophet portraying a time in the nation's future when, in the aftermath of divine judgment, the land will be filled with funerals. Grief and mourning will characterize the entire society: the people in the cities, the farmers, the professional mourners, and the workers in the vineyards.

Amos did not specify the Lord's method of punishment that would lead to such national devastation and loss. He did emphasize, through this morbid glimpse into the future, the certainty of God's judgment. "I will pass through the midst of you," God declared via Amos (v. 17b).

The expression is reminiscent of the last plague prior to the Exodus when the death angel passed through Egypt but "passed over" the Hebrews. This time, however, there would be no "passover." This time in Israel God would pass through.

The Day of the Lord (5:18-20)

Amos 5:18 contains the earliest reference to "the day of the Lord" in biblical literature. Later prophets referred to this concept quite frequently (Isa 2:12; 13:6-9; Jer 46:10; Ezek 7:19; 13:5; Joel 1:15; 2:1, 11, 31; 3:14; Zeph 1:7, 14-18). Even prior to Amos, however, "the day of the Lord" was already functioning as a powerful idea in the minds of many Israelites. For nearly all of the people of Israel, "the day of the Lord" represented a future time when God would intervene on Israel's behalf by bringing judgment and destruction upon Israel's enemies and by bringing blessings of honor and worldwide prominence on the Israelite nation.

The Israelites looked forward to this future day with eager anticipation. From their perspective, the long and prosperous reign of Jeroboam II that had led to economic and political revival for the nation was an indication that God was pleased with the northern kingdom. The coming "day of the Lord" would certainly be bright. Some scholars have even suggested that Israel officially celebrated this future "day of the Lord" at the beginning of each new year. In this way, each New Year's Day festival became a foretaste of the great day of the Lord when God would bless Israel and judge everyone else.[3] Such an annual celebration only enhanced Israel's longing for the day of the Lord. What a great and glorious day it would be!

"Not so," countered Amos. We can imagine the prophet addressing a crowd of people in one of the major cities such as Bethel. Perhaps it was even during the New Year's Day festival that Amos spoke. Whatever the time of his speaking, the content of his message was diametrically opposed to the cherished beliefs of the people.

Essentially, Amos proclaimed that the day of the Lord was coming but it would be a day of darkness and judgment for Israel. He was so convinced about the negative impact of the "day of the Lord" on Israel that he began his sermonette/oracle with the word "woe." The interjection "woe" was used in Amos' day as a cry of grief for those who died (1 Kgs 13:30; Jer 22:18; 34:5). "Woe" was a funeral word. Amos was already voicing a cry of grief over the coming "day of the Lord" that would bring destruction and death on Israel rather than the anticipated blessing and life. "Why would you desire such a day?" he asked (vv. 18, 20).

To insure that he had clearly made his point, Amos used some metaphors drawn from country and village life settings that stressed how negative and inescapable the day of the Lord would actually be (v. 19): like a man who escapes one danger (a lion) only to be overtaken by another dangerous predator (a bear), like a man who believes he is safe and secure in his home only to be bitten by a snake that has found its way into his house. The day of the Lord would be for Israel a day of "darkness not light"—a "day of gloom with no brightness in it."

Hated Worship; Needed Justice (5:21-24)

The Israelites had already heard Amos employ rather strong language in preaching against their worship services and rituals (4:4-5; 5:4-6), but this scarcely prepared them for what Amos proclaimed in the sermonette in verses 21-24—namely, that God hated and despised all that was done in the name of religion at the Israelite sanctuaries. Through exceedingly harsh language that undoubtedly shocked his hearers, Amos portrayed God as totally rejecting worship in the northern kingdom.

Notice how this divine rejection was presented. "I take no delight" in your solemn assemblies (v. 21) literally means "I will not smell" or "I don't like the smell of." "I will not look upon" your offerings (v. 22) and "I will not listen" to your music (v. 23) are other phrases that depict the Lord's displeasure with the worship of the Israelites. When considered together, these phrases indicate the extent to which God had rejected the activities at the Israelite sanctuaries. Indeed, the image was of God holding His nose, shutting His eyes, and closing His ears to Israel's religious services.[4]

But there is more. Amos listed seven different elements of Israel's worship that the Lord rejected (vv. 21-23). (1) The "festivals" refer to the three major annual feasts: passover, pentecost, and tabernacles or booths. (2) Regular worship services were the "solemn assemblies." (3) Burnt offerings were those in which the entire animal was consumed by fire. (4) Gifts of grain brought as a sacrifice were the "cereal offerings." (5) A "peace offering" (offering of well-being) entailed a meal in which the worshiper participated, with part of the sacrificed animal being eaten and part of it being burned. (6) The "noise" referred to the songs that were sung. (7) The "melody" signified the instrumental music that was played.

Was the listing of seven aspects of worship incidental or purposefully contrived? Recall that the number seven was used in biblical times to represent completeness or totality. Amos apparently enumerated seven elements of Israelite worship to demonstrate how totally and completely the Lord had rejected the worship of the northern kingdom.[5]

Why was Israelite worship not only unacceptable but also detestable to God? As Amos had already noted (4:4-5; 5:4-6), worship at Bethel, Gilgal and other sanctuaries had become an end in itself. The shrine and the worshiper had become more important than the one who was to be worshiped. Part of the divine rejection of Israelite worship was due to what was (and was not) happening inside the sanctuary.

Yet, a second major reason for the Lord's rejection of worship in Israel had to do with what was happening—or not happening—on the outside of the sanctuary walls. Once church was over, the Israelites acted as if they had never been. What happened (or should have happened) on the day of worship when church was in session had little or no bearing on what happened the other six days when church was out. Going to "church" on the Sabbath had no impact on how life was lived during the rest of the week.

In light of this unacceptable worship that God had rejected, Amos called for a lifestyle of justice and righteousness that the Lord would approve. This call comes in verse 24, the most well-known verse in Amos and the summary verse of the prophet's message.

We have already noted the close though not identical connection between righteousness and justice (see comments on 5:4-7). Righteousness is a relational term describing the will of God for the relationships within a community—how covenant people are expected to relate to the Lord, each other, and those outside the community itself. Justice has more of a legal flavor and refers to doing what is right in the law courts, which for Amos' audience met "in the gate." Practicing justice in the court system (and in other areas of society as well) was the process by which right relationships (that is, righteousness) could be restored within the community of God's people.

Yet, justice and righteousness were all but non-existent in the eighth-century B.C. Israel. Consequently, the Lord rejected Israel's worship. From God's perspective, even the most polished and well-planned worship services were meaningless if justice and righteousness were missing in the lives of the worshipers.

The image employed by Amos in verse 24 is significant. The supply and flow of water in the arid land of Israel was a life and death issue. Following a rain storm, river beds called wadis—which were normally dry—became the conduits through which life-giving water was distributed throughout the land. "Listen," Amos proclaimed to Israel, "justice and righteousness must be more than wadis that flow only on certain occasions, slow to a trickle at other times, and often dry up completely. Justice and righteousness are to be like rolling, surging streams of water that flow continuously."

Amos' call for justice and righteousness was not limited to the world of the eighth century B.C., God still expects doing what is right (justice) and having appropriate relationships with others (righteousness) to characterize today's covenant community: the church. If Amos were to speak to a contemporary audience of churchgoers on this issue, his message might be something like the following:

Evaluate your life for just a moment or two. Are you practicing justice? Are you doing what you know is right?

Some people in your peer group at school—even some that you consider to be your friends—are into drugs and substance abuse and experimenting with pre-marital sex. They have become party animals par excellence. They encourage you—perhaps even pressure you—to join them. You know that it is wrong, but you want to be included and liked. The question is: Will you practice justice? Will you do what is right?

Some things are going on at work or in your business that you know are not exactly ethical. Some expense accounts are being padded. Some taxable income is not being reported. There is some evidence of over-charging. Service rendered to the customer or workmanship that goes into the product is not exactly what it should be. People are not giving their best efforts, and some feel good about their ability to cheat the boss or shortchange the company. These folks are getting away with such practices. You are tempted to do likewise. After all, others are getting away with it. Why shouldn't you? But God asks of you daily: Will you practice justice? Will you do what is right?

Your life has become far too busy and hurried. Your schedule is incredibly jam packed. There is not a moment to spare. Work responsibilities, social commitments, and civic involvements pull you into all sorts of directions. You can't seem to turn down an offer, decline an invitation, or refuse an opportunity to make more money or climb just a little higher on the social ladder. But your children need a father. Your wife needs a husband. Your children need a mother. Your husband needs a wife. Your friend needs a friend. Your church needs a member. And you say that you are just too busy. But God asks: Are you really practicing justice? Are you doing what you know is right?

A person who has hurt you needs your forgiveness. You need to "bury the hatchet" and ask for forgiveness. Will you practice justice? Will you do what is right?

A project at the church or some ministry opportunity in the community calls for skills and talents that you have to share. You know that you need to use your talents in the Lord's work. But will you practice justice by doing what is right?

The offering plate is passed. The commitment card is mailed. The invitation is extended. The nominating committee calls. A fellow church member's life has been disrupted by tragedy or crisis. Will you practice justice? Will you do what is right?

All around you people (even those claiming to be God's people) seem to be more and more interested in money and materialism, status and prestige, power and self. People (even some in the church) are ignoring their families, being unfaithful to their marriages, neglecting their churches, ignoring their God. But the question that God raised long ago through Amos the prophet is still pertinent: Will you practice justice? Will you do what is right?

A Question Asked; Exile Predicted (5:25-27)

Many scholars regard these three verses as constituting a later addition to the original book of Amos, but there is no consensus on when, why, or by whom these verses may have been added. Since a close examination does reveal at least some connection between this passage and Amos 5:21-24 that immediately precedes it, there is some justification for treating verses 25-27 as part of the original text.

Verse 25 is a rhetorical question that was designed to be answered negatively: "No, our Israelite ancestors did not use sacrifices in their worship of God during the wilderness wandering experience." Amos undoubtedly followed a tradition that viewed the wilderness period of Israel's history as a time when the Israelites were faithful to God and the covenant (Hos 2:14-15; Jer 2:2; Amos 2:10).

Since sacrifices were not offered in the wilderness (due largely to the impracticality of such an endeavor), Amos seemingly argued that a right relationship with God and the acceptable worship of God did not necessarily depend upon such sacrifices or other ritual. Yet, a right relationship with God depends upon the presence of justice and righteousness in the lives of the worshipers (5:21-24). Right living is more important to the Lord than right ritual. Even the most extravagant sacrifices, if not accompanied by a right spirit, are unacceptable to the God of justice and righteousness.

The terms "Sakkuth" and "Kaiwan" in verse 26 are probably the names of two Assyrian gods who were connected with the star deity, Saturn. The original text of this verse is extremely difficult to reconstruct and interpret. It could be that Amos was issuing some type of threat against the Israelites who remained content on worshiping God

through external religious ritual devoid of the internal principles of justice and righteousness. Continuing such a practice would result in the Israelites being taken in captivity
where they would be forced to serve foreign deities such as
"Kaiwan" and "Sakkuth."

The threat that is implied in verse 26 is specifically
announced in verse 27. God would cause Israel to be carried away into captivity. Although the precise location of
Israel's imprisonment is not given, the phrase "beyond Damascus" strongly suggests Assyria (as does the mention of
the two Assyrian deities in verse 26). This chapter that
begins with a mock funeral concludes with an all-too-real
announcement of exile.

Woe for the Rich and Famous
(Amos 6)

"Alas." "Woe." The words were becoming all too familiar.
They were funeral words—words of mourning, words of
death, words of judgment, words of Amos. That southern
doomsday preacher was at it again.

Chapter 6 contains sermonettes of condemnation
and judgment that Amos directed against Israel's emerging
wealthy upper class. As these "new rich" became even richer, the poorer segment of Israel's population became even
poorer. Unfortunately, the increased financial portfolios of
the wealthy were often the direct result of the exploitation
and mistreatment of the poor. To make matters worse, Israel's "rich and famous" showed no concern for the plight of
the less fortunate (2:6). Such glaring examples of injustice
and unrighteousness did not go unnoticed, nor would they
go unpunished by God.

Declaring God's displeasure was once again Amos' task. There is scarcely any way to mistake the meaning of the prophetic message as given in the sermonettes of chapter 6. It begins with a funeral cry (v. 1), continues with the prediction of exile (v. 7), goes on to speak of a wave of death that would engulf the nation (v. 9), and concludes by identifying the Lord's method (exile) of judgment (v. 13).

Delusions of Grandeur (6:1-7)

Once again Amos used funeral language to convey God's message to Israel (5:1-2, 16-17). Beginning his sermonette with the word "woe" was comparable to beginning a contemporary speech by reading an obituary. Whenever people of Amos' day heard the pronouncement "woe," they understood that a death had occurred. "Who died?" must have been a question that automatically surfaced in their minds when they heard Amos introduce his speech with "woe."

Amos wasted no time in identifying the "deceased." His "woe" was directed to Israel's aristocratic elite, the nation's leaders whom Amos (with tongue in cheek) called "the notables of the first of the nations" (v. 1). These arrogant individuals evidently regarded themselves as belonging to the "first families" of Israel. Their societal status caused them to develop a false sense of national security and self-sufficiency that Amos described as being "at ease in Zion" and "feeling secure on Mount Samaria."

Mistakenly, they bought into the popular motion that God would always protect Jerusalem (Zion) regardless of how the Lord's people behaved. Although it was located in Judah, the presence of Zion/Jerusalem provided a feeling of security that fueled arrogant and snobbish attitudes.

And if having Jerusalem/Zion were not enough, there was always the well-fortified natural fortress of Samaria, their capital city, which many Israelites viewed as impregnable.

To underscore the incredible arrogance of his audience, Amos apparently quoted the elite leaders of Israel in verse 2. "Why just look at the cities of Calneh, Hamath, and Gath," the bragging leaders told their Israelite constituents. "They are undoubtedly highly regarded and successful cities, but they pale in comparison to the cities of Israel. We're the best!"

Verse 2 is just one of several instances when Amos repeated or quoted his hearers (2:12; 4:1; 5:14; 6:13; 7:16; 8:5-6, 14; 9:10). The "we're-better-than-they-are" bragging of Israel's leaders focused on three cities: the two northern city-states, Hamath in upper Syria and Calneh near Carchemish, and the Philistine city of Gath. Through the utilization of this rather haughty quote, Amos condemned the conceited attitude of Israel's leaders by using their own words against them.

Returning to his own words in verse 3, Amos chided his listeners for neglecting to take seriously his message of coming judgment. Indeed, these elite leaders of Israel were so arrogantly secure about themselves that they continuously postponed ("put far away") any consideration whatsoever of the coming day of the Lord even possibly being for Israel an "evil day" (5:18-20). Their "live-for-the-moment" philosophy resulted in the further exploitation of the poor and defenseless persons in Israel society—an increasingly "rich-get-richer-poor-get-poorer" scenario that all too easily becomes a powder keg for violence, as we know it.

The funeral talk continues in verses 4-6, with Amos shifting slightly from a focus on the arrogant and self-indulgent leadership styles of Israel's aristocratic elite to a vivid description of the luxurious lifestyles that these rich "first families" of Israel enjoyed. According to Amos, this affluent lifestyle included sleeping and lounging on expensive furniture, feasting on prime cuts of meat, listening to dinner music, singing idle songs and participating in sing-alongs as a form of after dinner entertainment, drinking wine in bowls instead of the customary goblet or cup, and liberally anointing themselves with expensive perfume.

As the prophet portrayed such an exceedingly opulent standard of living, it was difficult to avoid making comparisons with the plight of Israel's poor. Yet, as incredulous as it seems, Israel's elite and wealthy citizens were so caught up in the enjoyment of their affluence that they were not even "grieved over the ruin of Joseph!"—that is, they did not even give consideration to the deteriorating social and economic welfare of the poor of Israel who remained part of Israel's covenant family despite not being treated as such.

The use of seven verbs in the description of the lifestyle of Israel's wealthy class is intriguing. According to Amos 6:4-6, these verbs include lie, lounge, eat, sing, improvise, drink, and anoint.[6] Since seven is the biblical number signifying "completeness" or "wholeness," could the utilization of seven verbs in this context have some type of special significance? Could Amos be saying that the rich Israelites were so completely and totally enamored by their riches that they completely and totally became indifferent toward the needs and struggles of their fellow Israelites. Surely people in our more sophisticated and educated day would never become so totally and completely enthralled by luxury, would they? Would we?

With a loud and emphatic "therefore" (v. 7), Amos announced the judgment that would fall on Israel. The funeral talk (woe) in verse 1 was necessitated by the nation's "death" of exile predicted in verse 7. Notice how skillfully Amos employed irony in his description of Israel's exile: the "notables of the first of the nations" (Israel's leading "first families," v. 1) would be the first of the Israelites to be sent into exile (v. 7).

The Certainty of Judgment (6:8-14)

How certain was the coming divine judgment of exile upon Israel? So certain that Amos boldly asserted how the Lord had taken an oath regarding the matter. To "swear by himself" means that God had put the very essence of Godhood and divine integrity on the line (4:2; 8:7). If God had anything to do with the announced exile (and the Lord ultimately had everything to do with it), then judgment on Israel by exile would occur.

The "pride of Jacob" (v. 8) refers to the cocky attitude of arrogance and security that characterized Israel's leaders (6:1-3). Such self-centered sinful pride had pushed Israel beyond the "saturation point" of divine tolerance; judgment was irrevocable. In the northern kingdom, God had been replaced by selfish pride as the center of Israelite living. With what do we dare replace God as the central focus of our lives?

Verses 9-10 may have originally been part of a separate sermonette. As indicated by the NRSV translation, these verses are prose, while all of the immediately preceding and succeeding verses of Amos' sermonettes have been preserved in poetic form. The placement of the verses in their present location by either Amos or his disciple editors was surely due to the devastating post-judgment scene that they portrayed. Though difficult to translate, the general meaning of the verses can be ascertained.

Verse 9 presupposes that some type of horrible judgment had already happened. Those who somehow survived the first wave of disaster ("ten people" who "remain in one house") would not survive for long. The scene in verse 10 is even more gruesome.

Evidently, there were many dead bodies lying in the cities following the divine judgment. A designated relative, in Hebrew culture the one assigned the responsibility of burying his relatives, entered a house to dispose of the corpses of his kinspeople. That he is referred to as "one who burns the dead" may suggest that the bodies were to be cremated, possibly because the cause of death was some type of contagious pestilence. Upon entering the house, this designated relative discovered a survivor. When the survivor called out that no one else remained, the designated relative called for silence. He realized that divine judgment had struck and feared that even the incidental mention of the name of the Lord might somehow cause another wave of divine wrath to be unleashed.

The belief that none other than the Lord brought this disaster upon Israel is reinforced by verse 11. God commanded this destruction to occur. Based on the content of the verse, the judgment could have been carried out through an earthquake or invading military force. Whatever the method, both small and large homes were "shattered to bits." No distinction between modest or extravagant households was made. God's judgment was thorough and complete.

Verse 12 presents Amos once again drawing from the influence of wisdom literature (1:3; 3:3-6; 3:12). The prophet assumed the role of a wisdom teacher in an attempt to persuade the Israelites to recognize how absurd their behavior and conduct had become. Specifically, Amos asked two ridiculous rhetorical questions: Does one gallop horses over rocks? Does a person try to plow the sea with oxen? The answer to both questions is "no" since such actions would be utterly absurd. Yet, just as absurd were the unjust and unrighteous actions of the Israelites.

As Amos noted time and time again, the inhabitants of the northern kingdom claimed the privileges of being God's covenant people without accepting the covenant responsibilities of living lives characterized by justice and righteous. "That," said Amos, "is really absurd." The final two verses of chapter 6 juxtapose the arrogant pride of Israel (v. 13) with the Lord's plan for judging the Israelites (v. 14). As an indication of its self-sufficiency and power, Israel pointed to a successful military victory in which the towns of Lo-debar and Karnaim were captured by the troops of Jeroboam II (v. 13; 2 Kgs 14:25). Yet, Amos understood that this relatively minor military success would be short-lived. We can imagine that Amos even sarcastically reminded his hearers that the meaning of Lo-debar is literally "nothing."

At any rate, Amos closed this sermonette by countering Israel's arrogant pride with the announcement that God was raising up a nation to defeat and oppress the northern kingdom. Although this nation that would act as God's agent of judgment is not specifically identified, there is little question that Amos was speaking of Assyria.

The two geographical sites mentioned in verse 14 are significant. Lebo-hamath was regarded as the northernmost boundary of Jeroboam II's kingdom. The Wadi Arabah, sometimes recognized as the Brook Zered at the south part of the Dead Sea, was the southern limit of Israel during the time of Jeroboam II. "From Lebo-hamath to the Wadi Arabah" was Amos' way of emphasizing that God's coming judgment against Israel via the military conquest of the Lord's already selected nation (Assyria) would be all encompassing and complete.

The end of chapter 6 also brings the "words" section of the book of Amos to a close. Through sermon and sermonettes, Amos creatively delivered God's message calling for the establishment of justice and righteousness in a "surface only" religious society where injustice and unrighteousness prevailed. Even when the divine message that he felt called to proclaim seemed especially harsh and judgmental, Amos would still not back down. He boldly preached to and against Israel's political, judicial, religious, and business leaders. Both men and women were the targets of his prophetic pronouncements. Under conviction from God, Amos had a word from the Lord, and he had to preach it!

Questions for Reflection

1. From the perspective of Israel, what did being God's chosen people mean? From the perspective of Amos?

2. What was the "day of the Lord"? How did Amos and his Israelite audience differ in their interpretations of this concept?

3. Why is the phrase "in the gate" significant for a study of Amos?

4. What is the relationship between justice and righteousness?

6. Why did God find worship in the northern kingdom so displeasing?

Notes

[1]James Limburg, *Hosea-Micah*, "Interpretation: A Biblical Commentary for Teaching and Preaching" (Atlanta: John Knox Press, 1988) 93.

[2]Ibid., 95.

[3]Bernhard W. Anderson, *Understanding the Old Testament*, 2d. ed. (Englewood Cliffs NJ: Prentice-Hall, Inc., 1966) 235.

[4]John C. Shelley, "Amos," *Mercer Commentary on the Bible* (Macon GA: Mercer University Press, 1995) 751.

[5]Limburg, 104-105.

[6]Ibid., 111.

Chapter 3

Visions of Judgment
A Clash over Authority
A Hint of Hope

7:1–9:15

"The phenomenon of vision was a constitutive
element in the prophetic experience. Prophets
received their call and were told the plans of
Yahweh through visions."
                              —James Luther Mays
                          Amos (Old Testament Library)

Amos 7:1–9:15 forms the second major part of the book of
Amos. Known as the visions of Amos, this portion of the
book contains five visions that Amos experienced (7:1-3;
7:4-6; 7:7-9; 8:1-3; 9:1-4). In addition to the five visions, this
block of scripture also records several significant "non-
visionary" passages including Amos' confrontation with
Amaziah the priest (7:10-17), additional sermonettes against
Israel (8:4-14; 9:5-10), and a prophetic epilogue of future
hope (9:11-15).

Four Visions (7:1-9; 8:1-3)

The Old Testament reports the visionary experiences of numerous prophets (Isa 6:1; Jer 1:11-14; Ezek 1:1, Nahum 1:1). Through these visions, God communicated with individuals who often felt compelled to serve the Lord in specific ways following such visionary encounters. We might think of visions as being somewhat like dreams but usually occurring while the recipient is conscious. Exactly "how" visions happened or even exactly "what" visions were, however, are questions that scripture does not fully address.

The biblical writers seemed quite comfortable in allowing some of the mystery associated with visions to remain mystery. More important than the "how" or the "what" of visionary experiences was the affirmation that God used visions as a means of communicating with and sometimes extending a call to human beings.

The visions of Amos were evidently highly intensive personal encounters with God through which Amos became convinced of the Lord's coming judgment against Israel. We cannot determine precisely when Amos experienced these visions. Perhaps it was during his shepherding days in Judah when he received God's call to travel northward to Israel and preach. Notice that Amos 1:1 declares: "The words of Amos, who was among the shepherds of Tekoa, which he *saw* concerning Israel. . . ."

Perhaps Amos experienced these visions in one initial setting, or maybe they occurred periodically throughout his ministry as part of an ongoing call from God. Whenever he experienced them, God used them to convince Amos of divine doomsday judgment that was about to strike Israel.

The first four of the five Amos visions follow a basic pattern that was also utilized by other prophets in reporting their vision experiences (Jer 1:11-14; 24:1-2; Zech 1:20-21; 5:1-4). This pattern is as follows: (1) an introductory formula—"This is what the Lord God showed me"; (2) a description of the content of the vision—"Behold" (RSV) followed by a report of what was seen or heard; and (3) a dialogue between the prophet and the Lord. The fifth vision (9:1-4) does not adhere to this basic pattern but differs in form, content, and length from the first four visions.

For purposes of analysis, the first four visions can be categorized into two pairs. The first pair (7:1-3; 7:4-6) is often referred to as "event-visions." So obvious is the meaning of the event portrayed in each "event vision" that no interpretation is given or needed. In each "event vision" account, Amos initiates the dialogue with God and intercedes on behalf of Israel.

The second pair of visions (7:7-9; 8:1-3) is known as "word-play visions." As these "word-play visions" unfold, an interpretation is needed and given. In each "word-play vision" account, God initiates the dialogue with Amos, interprets the vision, and announces the divine judgment. In contrast to the first two visions, Amos does not intercede on behalf of the people following visions three and four.

Vision #1: Locusts and Prophetic Intercession (7:1-3)

In the first vision, Amos saw the Lord forming locusts that devoured the country's crops. This envisioned plague of locusts came at a very critical time when the late plantings of spring crops were just beginning to sprout. (The king had already claimed the first cutting of the spring crops as a type of national tax.) Since the dry season of summer was about to begin, growing additional crops would not be possible until the following season. Losing the late plantings of spring crops would almost certainly result in famine.

Locust plagues occurred rather frequently in Amos' part of the world. Such devastating locust swarms were often regarded as plagues of God (Exod 10:12ff; Deut 28:38, 42; Joel 1; Amos 4:9). Amos needed no interpretation when he saw this vision. Just as the locusts had come and destroyed the crucial spring crops, the Lord was about to come and destroy the nation of Israel.

Amos took the initiative and interceded on behalf of Israel. He asked God to forgive Israel (Jacob) because the nation was so "small" that it could not survive the coming judgment. How ironic that the Israelites of Amos' day who arrogantly regarded themselves as "big" and invulnerable were characterized as "small" by Amos when the prophet interceded on their behalf!

God responded favorably to Amos' intercession and "relented" (v. 3). The RSV and KJV translate this phrase "The Lord repented concerning this." When used in reference to God, "repent" or "relent" certainly does not suggest any wrongdoing or sin on the part of the Lord. Rather, the relenting or repenting of God indicates that the Lord is so personally involved with people that there is a sense of divine sorrow whenever judgment becomes necessary.

Several Old Testament writers used this concept of God repenting/relenting to indicate that the Lord cares about people, answers the prayers of people, and is open to "changing His mind" if there is a noted change in the lives of people (Gen 6:7; 1 Sam 15:29, 35; Jonah 3:9; Joel 2:14). The Lord's relenting gave Israel a reprieve. Yet, Amos probably realized that the reprieve would be temporary unless the Israelites genuinely changed and repented.

Vision #2: Fire and Prophetic Intercession (7:4-6)

What Amos saw in the second vision was a "shower of fire" that had already devoured the "great deep"—the waters under the earth (Gen 7:11; Ps 36:6)—and was in the process of destroying the land. This fire could refer to a drought caused by the scorching heat that literally dries up all of a region's water sources. More than likely, however, the vision of this devastating fire is a reference to the fires of war—the fires set by soldiers as they invade and occupy another country.

The perceptive Amos immediately understood the message of the devastating vision. Israel was on the threshold of destruction. Once again, the prophet interceded for Jacob/Israel because the nation was so small. This time Amos did not ask God's forgiveness of Israel. Sensing the urgency of the situation, Amos cut to the core of the matter by begging the Lord to stop the coming judgment. And the Lord's response? Once more, a stay of execution was granted.

The accounts of the first two visions demonstrate Amos' willingness not only to speak for God but also to fulfill another sometimes overlooked prophetic role: the role of an intercessor for people (Exod 32:30-34; 1 Sam 12:23; 1 Kgs 17:20-21). The intercession by Amos on behalf of Israel had the effect of delaying God's judgment. Yet, as sincere as Amos' intercession was, intercessory intervention by the prophet alone could not ultimately stop the Lord's judgment. Only genuine repentance by the people could cause the divine punishment to be renounced totally. In effect, Amos' intercession for the northern kingdom bought the people a little time—time to repent, which unfortunately passed by without any repentance.

Vision #3: The Plumb Line (7:7-9)

The third vision is the first of two "word-play visions."
Amos saw the Lord standing by a wall and holding a
plumb line, an instrument consisting of a cord and weight
whose function was to measure if the wall of a building
was vertically straight. This visionary image portrayed God
as some kind of construction crew foreman testing a wall
to determine if it has been built according to acceptable
standards.

Unlike the meanings of the first two visions, however, the meaning of this third vision was not obvious to
Amos. Consequently, the Lord took the initiative and provided the correct interpretation for this vision:

> "What do you see, Amos?" God asked. "A
> plumb line," answered Amos. "Don't you see,
> Amos?" the Lord explained. "I'm about to set a
> plumb line in the midst of my people Israel. I
> will never again pass them by. They no longer
> measure up to my standards for a covenant peo-
> ple. Like a crooked wall that needs to be torn
> down, my people Israel need to be and will be
> destroyed."

Following the Lord's interpretation, Amos began to
get the picture. The meaning of the vision was so devastating that he did not even attempt to intercede on Israel's
behalf. Amos finally understood. Israel did not measure up
to God's standard. Certainly judgment through this third
vision had been pronounced. The nation would be destroyed. Even the once-vaunted high places of worship and
holy sanctuaries would be laid waste. Not only the reign of

Jeroboam II, but the entire Jeroboam dynasty would be brought to an end.

Amos "got" the meaning of this third vision alright. His only response was silence. Even such silence served as an ominous sign of what lay ahead. For many people, the future held the silence of exile; for the nation, the silence of death.

Vision #4: A Basket of Summer Fruit (8:1-3)

The account of the fourth vision begins with God showing Amos a basket of summer fruit. In Hebrew, the word for summer fruit is *qayits*. When the Lord asked Amos what he saw, the prophet responded: "a basket of *qayits*." Then God provided the interpretation for this word-play vision by declaring, "The end (*qets* in Hebrew) has come upon my people Israel. I will never again pass them by."

Hearing the divine word-play involving *qayits* and *qets*, Amos understood the devastating meaning of this vision. No longer would the Lord's threatened judgment "pass by" the people of Israel as God's death angel had once "passed over" their Israelite ancestors (8:3b; 7:8b, Exod 12:23; Amos 5:17). God's judgment would pass through the midst of the northern kingdom. Songs of worship and joy would be transformed to songs of mourning and laments, and corpses would be found throughout the nation. Finally, the sound of silence—the sound of death—would prevail.

With visions three and four, the finality of Israel's fate became a certainty for Amos—no more prophetic intercessions, no more divine reprieves. Judgment was imminent and the "day of the Lord" at hand. The end (*qets*) for Israel had arrived.

Amaziah and Amos
Institutional versus Experiential Religion
(Amos 7:10-17)

Located between the third and fourth vision accounts is
one of the most unforgettable scenes in all of the Old Testament: the confrontation between Amos and Amaziah the
priest. This biographical prose narrative actually interrupts
the logical flow of the text from the third vision (7:7-9) to
the fourth vision (8:1-3). The editors of the book of Amos
apparently placed this biographical narrative at this particular location because of the connection between the content
of 7:9 and 7:10-11, both of which refer to the threat against
King Jeroboam and his dynasty.

Who was this Amaziah with whom Amos had such
a memorable confrontation? He was the chief priest/senior
pastor of the royal sanctuary at Bethel, the religious capital
of the northern kingdom. Since Bethel was the royal sanctuary, the king and his family worshiped there. Amaziah was
Jeroboam II's pastor/priest—literally! Amaziah and the rest
of the ministerial staff at the royal sanctuary were on the
royal payroll of Jeroboam II. The king was not only a member of Amaziah's "church"; the king was Amaziah's boss!

As the head priest at the royal sanctuary, Amaziah's
chief concern was to keep the royal court happy. No wonder Amaziah became concerned and more than just a little
ruffled when Amos arrived at Bethel, criticizing the worship and passing judgment against King Jeroboam himself!
This just would not do. Amos was upsetting the status quo.
If left unchecked, this fiery southern orator would also
disrupt the ongoing operations of the sanctuary and

undoubtedly continue to declare harsh words of judgment against the nation and the king. Amaziah had to do something. He devised a plan that was designed to eliminate Amos and get operations at the royal sanctuary running smoothly again.

Before considering Amaziah's plan, however, consider the following description of contemporary pastors by Eugene Peterson that—when slightly altered—offers genuine insight into religious figures such as Amaziah:

> The pastors of America [the priests of eighth-century B.C. Israel] have metamorphosed [been transformed] into a company of shopkeepers, and the shops they keep are churches [sanctuaries]. They are preoccupied with shopkeeper's concerns—how to keep the customers happy . . . how to package the goods so that the customers will lay out more money.
>
> Some of them are very good shopkeepers. They attract a lot of customers, pull in great sums of money, develop splendid reputations. Yet, it is still shopkeeping; religious shopkeeping, to be sure, but shopkeeping all the same.[1]

The institutional religion of Amaziah had transformed the priest into a shopkeeper. The shop he was determined to keep was the Bethel sanctuary, the well-kept royal sanctuary that was threatened by the ministry of Amos.

The Plan of Amaziah (7:10-13)

Amaziah's plan was two-fold in nature: (1) reporting the disruptive and threatening ministry of Amos to King

Jeroboam II and (2) confronting Amos face to face with a gag order and an expulsion decree. The decision to report Amos' activities to Jeroboam II is not surprising. We can imagine that regular reporting to the king was included in Amaziah's job description. Yet, this was not just a monthly report; it was an urgent news bulletin. This Amos character was guilty of conspiracy and treason. He had declared that Jeroboam would be "killed by the sword" (7:9, 11) and the people of Israel would be sent into exile (4:3; 5:27; 6:7; 7:17).

The report of Amaziah to the king was not 100 percent accurate. At best, it misrepresented Amos in two major ways.[2] First, Amaziah reported how Amos had prefaced his threatening messages against Jeroboam II and Israel with the phrase "for thus Amos has said." A major characteristic of Amos' preaching was the prophet's determination to proclaim not his own words but the message of God. The phrase "thus says the Lord," not "thus Amos has said," permeated the prophet's preaching.

Amaziah also misrepresented Amos to the king by reporting only a selected portion of the prophet's message. Granted, Amos as the Lord's spokesperson had announced God's coming punishment upon Israel, but Amaziah omitted the reasons that Amos gave for the Lord's judgment. In his report to Jeroboam II, Amaziah never mentioned Amos' accusations regarding the numerous examples of injustice and unrighteousness in Israelite society.

Was this because Amaziah secretly agreed that Amos was right? Did Amaziah neglect reporting Amos' claim to be preaching the message of God because he himself wondered if Amos' preaching might possibly be of God? Was Amaziah so committed to pleasing the king and so loyal to institutional religion that he refrained from telling the king the truth?

Phase two of Amaziah's plan for dealing with Amos called for a personal confrontation with this troublesome southern prophet. We assume that Amaziah had Jeroboam II's backing and blessing to do what he did in this confrontation—namely, to ban Amos from ever again preaching at the Bethel sanctuary and to tell Amos to go back to Judah (vv. 12-13).

Amaziah addressed Amos as a "seer," a term that should not necessarily be interpreted in a negative way. Indeed, the terms "seer" and "prophet" (*nabi'*) could be used interchangably (2 Kgs 17:13; Amos 7:12, 14). Rather than being scornful and hateful toward Amos, the primary goal of Amaziah was apparently to get rid of Amos. He did not care if Amos continued to prophesy as long as he no longer prophesied at or around Bethel. He simply did not want to have to deal with Amos, the issues he raised, or the coming judgment he predicted.

The double emphasis on "there" in verse 12 is telling. "If I can somehow get Amos to go back *there* to Judah and to prophesy back *there*," reasoned Amaziah, "then I won't have to be bothered with him *here* at Bethel." Having Amos back "there" in Judah would make it easier for Amaziah to keep Jeroboam II happy by keeping operations at the Bethel sanctuary running smoothly. "After all," Amaziah declared in urging Amos to return home, "Bethel . . . is the *king's sanctuary*, and it is a *temple of the kingdom*."

The Response of Amos (7:14-15)

Amos responded to Amaziah's remarks by clarifying his vocation and calling. "I am no prophet, nor a prophet's son," he declared. What did Amos mean by this statement that seems quite puzzling when one considers all of the prophesying that Amos had done? Apparently, Amos meant that he was not one of the many professional prophets who earned a living by prophesying. These professionals included the "sons of the prophets" who were members of professional prophetic guilds located in religious centers such as Bethel and Gilgal (1 Kgs 20:35; 2 Kgs 2:3-4; 4:1, 38). There were other bands of prophets who tended to travel and prophesy throughout the land (1 Sam 10:5, 10; 19:20) and groups of prophets associated with the royal court who were evidently on the king's payroll (1 Kgs 22:6, 10-12).

"I'm not one of those professional prophets who prophesy for profit," Amos said in response to Amaziah. To underscore the fact that he was not a professional prophet on anyone's payroll, Amos declared what he did for a living: he raised sheep and cared for sycamore trees. In fact, while working as a shepherd God called him to go and prophesy to Israel. And go Amos did, not because he was on anyone's payroll but because he was convinced that the Lord was calling him to go and preach "thus says the Lord" messages of judgment against Israel. Amos was not some paid, high-powered, professional prophet. He was a layperson who was called by God.

The Judgment on Amaziah (7:16-17)

The confrontation between priest and prophet concluded with Amos' announcement of God's judgment against Amaziah and his family. This is the only time in the book of Amos that one of Amos' oracles is spoken to an individual. What a horribly harsh judgment it would be! Amaziah's wife would be forced into prostitution, his children killed, his land divided up to become the property of outsiders, and his fellow Israelites sent into exile. And the divine judgment on Amaziah himself? Evidently, he too would be exiled and die in a foreign land.

Following the pronouncement by Amos of God's judgment, we hear no more of Amaziah. We assume that he continued keeping shop at Bethel until the time that the prophecies of judgment announced by Amos came true. His legacy of an external, institutionalized religion has hindered the effectiveness of God's followers throughout the centuries and continues to impinge negatively on many of the Lord's followers today. It is the legacy of a religion that always favors the status quo and never favors change even when change is necessary. The legacy of a religion whose rituals and traditions that have been designed to enhance the worship of God have become more important than God. It is the legacy of a religion required to refrain from criticizing itself—the legacy of a religion that ultimately becomes responsible to a power other than the Lord.

How fortunate that, in addition to the legacy of Amaziah, we have the legacy of an Amos—the legacy of a religion that is experiential in nature, the legacy of a religion that is based upon God's call, the legacy of a religion that emphasizes responsibility as well as privilege, the legacy of a religion that calls for "Monday–Saturday" living as well as "gathering-for-church-on-Sunday" worship, the legacy of a religion that is ever alert to the Jeroboams of life who compete for our ultimate allegiance.[3]

More Sermonettes against Israel
(8:4-14)

Although located within the "visions" section of Amos, the bulk of chapter 8 is actually non-visionary material. The "hear this" introduction (8:4) introduces the last of four collections of sermonettes that are featured in the book of Amos (also 3:1, 4:1, 5:1).

Judgment on Greedy Merchants (8:4-8)

In many respects, the sermonette in 8:4-8 against Israel's businessmen parallels Amos' previous sermonette against Israel's "cows-of-Bashan" women (4:1-5). Both sermonettes begin with the "hear this" formula (4:1; 8:4). Both develop the theme of Israel's mistreatment of the "poor" and "needy" (4:1; 8:4). The women are portrayed as urging their husbands to make more money in order to support their lavish lifestyles, even if doing so meant cheating the poor (4:1c). At least some of the husbands of these women were the merchants and businessmen portrayed in chapter 8 as those who cheated the poor in order to make more money to support the luxurious lifestyles their wives had come to expect (8:4-6).

Both sermonettes depict the Lord as "having sworn" that judgment would fall on the ones oppressing the poor (4:2; 8:7). Finally, both sermonettes describe the divine judgment that would strike each respective group (4:3; 8:8). These parallel accounts demonstrate that both the women and men of Israel would be held accountable for their gross injustices against the poor.

Amos specifically charged the businessmen with greed. The "new moon" (v. 5) refers to one of ancient Israel's religious festivals that was held at the beginning of every lunar month (1 Sam 20:5; 2 Kgs 4:23; Hos 2:11). No work was done on the "new moon" or the sabbath. These were holy days to be celebrated at the sanctuary. Yet, even as Israel's merchants went through the external motions of religious piety, they were inwardly thinking about their places of business and how much money they could make as soon as the holy days were over and they could open their shops again (v. 5).

These merchants were also charged with cheating their customers. The ephah (v. 5b) was a dry measure roughly equivalent to a bushel. By using an undersized "ephah basket," the merchant would short-change the customers. The shekel (v. 5b) was a weight used on scales in weighing grain. When the shekel was "great" or heavy, the customer was treated unfairly. Other charges brought against the merchants by Amos include "buying" the poor as slaves when they could not pay their bills and selling the wheat chaff and trash as if it were clean grain (v. 6).

The Lord would hold the merchants accountable for each of their unjust deeds and sins against the poor (v. 7). Since God took an oath that divine judgment would fall on Israel, coming judgment was assured. Amos described the devastating nature of God's coming judgment on Israel by describing its effects as those of an earthquake (v. 8; 2:13; 3:14; 9:1).

"On That Day": God's Judgment (8:9-10)

The expression "on that day" is a signal that Amos was speaking about the "day of the Lord" (5:18-20; 8:13; 9:11).

Israel had anticipated this day being a time of rejoicing when God would overthrow its enemies and elevate its status to "number one" among all of the nations of the earth. Amos had previously declared, however, that this day would not be a day of celebration at all but a day of judgment—a day of darkness and gloom (5:18, 20).

In the sermonette in 8:9-10, Amos reiterated his contention that in the "day of the Lord" ("that day"), God would send judgment and punishment upon Israel. The use of the "divine I" four times in these verses underscores the certainty of judgment by the Lord. The consequences of this "day" would be fatal, with weeping, lamentation, the wearing of sackcloth, and the shaving of heads—all rituals observed when an Israelite died (Isa 15:2ff; Micah 1:16). Yet, it would be worse than the death of an individual, even worse than the death of an only son. "This day" would represent the death of the nation.

More Words of Judgment (8:11-14)

In 8:11-14, Amos employs a different image to describe the consequences of the coming day of the Lord. The image is of a famine, not a "famine of bread" nor a "thirst for water," but a famine of hearing the word of God (v. 11)—the total absence of God from Israel.

The Israelites had failed to "seek the Lord while the Lord could be found." They had opted for increased material wealth and selfish dishonest lifestyles rather than choosing to implement justice and righteousness in their lives. Time and time again, God had implored them to "seek me and live" (Amos 5:6, 14), but the people had continuously chosen to reject God and so would die when the "day of the Lord" arrived.

Amos continued with this grim judgment scene by depicting the Israelites wandering aimlessly throughout the land seeking the word of the Lord (v. 12). The last "seek me and live" from God had been offered. The final reprieve delaying judgment had been given. For Israel, the Lord was not at hand; the time of inexorable judgment was near.

Even the strongest, most youthful Israelites could not live with the absence of God (v. 13). Turning to seek guidance from other gods (v. 14) proved futile. For Israel, the "day of the Lord" would be the time of God's absence. The judgment would be too final and oh so certain: "They shall fall and never rise again" (v. 14).

Another Vision, Another Doxology
Other Judgments
(Amos 9:1-10)

As the book of Amos draws to a close, the prophet's picture of God's coming judgment against the northern kingdom grows even darker. As Amos ended his ministry to Israel, seemingly he wanted to do everything in his power to convey the message of God to his Israelite audience. He desired no one to misunderstand.

Israel's sins against God, especially in its failure to practice justice and righteousness, had surpassed the saturation point. For "three generations of Israel," the Lord had been gracious, offered forgiveness, granted reprieves, and withheld judgment. Yet, the Israelites had not responded to God's graciousness. Justice and righteousness had not been practiced. A sinful point of no return had indeed been surpassed. The "fourth generation of Israel" had come. God's judgment against Israel was soon to occur.

Amos did not want anyone to misunderstand his message of judgment and doom, so he (or his editorial disciples) took several steps in the final chapter to assure that the message would be communicated and conveyed.

The Fifth Vision: The Lord beside the Altar (9:1-4)

The fifth and final vision in the book of Amos breaks from the pattern of the first four (7:1-9; 8:1-3). Rather than emphasizing the vision, 9:1-4 briefly describes a vision of the Lord standing beside an altar (v. 1a) and then focuses the rest of the account on a divine speech (vv. 1b-4). Amos heard God's commandment that the sanctuary be destroyed. Perhaps such destruction was from an earthquake since the sanctuary columns that God commanded to be struck caused the roof to collapse and the foundations of the building to "shake" (v. 1). Many of the worshipers were killed, with the survivors facing death by the "sword" of the Lord, a probable reference to warfare. The vision is one of total decimation and judgment, with no escape.

The vision account could have ended at this juncture, its task of describing complete destruction fulfilled. Yet, two additional means are employed to leave the listening and reading audience with no doubt whatsoever as to the thoroughness of God's devastating judgment. First, in what has been described as Psalm 139 in reverse, great care is taken to show that there was no place where Israel could flee to escape God's punishment. Five allegedly "God-proof" hiding places are enumerated: Sheol, the lowest cosmic depth; heaven, the highest cosmic height; Mount Carmel, a high earthly mountain with numerous hiding places; the bottom of the sea; and exile. Yet, in each of these hiding places, God would search out and destroy.

The second way the vision demonstrates the totality of God's judgment is through the enumeration of seven specific acts that the Lord would carry out against the guilty Israelites: "I will slay . . . my hand take . . . I will bring them down . . . I will search out . . . take them . . . I will command the sea-serpent . . . I will command the sword . . . (9:1-4).[4] Recall that seven is the biblical number for totality and completeness. The fifth and final vision is brought into focus. Israel could expect God's judgment to be total and complete.

A Third Doxology
(9:5-6)

Amos 9:5-6 is the third of three doxologies, all of which may have originally derived from a single hymn of praise. The third doxology affirms God's creative power (v. 5), majesty (v. 6a), and control over nature (v. 6b) Why incorporate a doxology into a scripture passage dealing with judgment? To affirm that the God of creation was more than powerful enough to carry out the devastating judgment that had been pronounced against Israel. Indeed, this creator God could touch the "earth" and cause it to "melt" as well as cause the land to "rise and sink" like the Nile River (v. 5; see the earthquake description in 8:8). For doomsday-oriented Amos, even a doxology of praise could become a hymn of judgment.

Final Words about the Certainty of Judgment (9:7-10)

Many scholars view these verses as constituting the close of the book of Amos. Verses 11-15 along with verse 8b are often attributed to the hand of a later editor (see the epilogue). What did Amos want to accomplish through his final words in 9:7-10? He wanted to emphasize one more time that God's coming judgment of destruction on Israel was certain. He wanted his audience in the northern kingdom to "get it." Yet, Israel never "got it," at least not until after the nation's fall in 722 B.C. Then, in retrospect, the Israelites undoubtedly remembered Amos' messages and thought: "So that's what Amos meant. He was right after all!"

Still, Amos was persistent in his "certainty-of-judgment" preaching. Once more he combated the widely held belief that Israel's covenant with the Lord granted the nation some type of special immunity from God's judgment (v. 7; 3:1-2). "Not so!" protested Amos. Then the fiery prophet utilized two rhetorical questions to demonstrate that no nation—not even Israel—could claim a "favored nation" status that exempted it from God's judgment.

Amos used the first rhetorical question to compare Israel to the Ethiopians: "Are you not like the Ethiopians to me, O people of Israel? says the Lord" (v. 7). The meaning of the question is clear. In God's sight, Ethiopians and Israelites had equal status. Next Amos employed the second rhetorical question to emphasize God's active involvement in the histories of the Philistines and the Arameans, two of Israel's longstanding enemies. Indeed, God had delivered these nations through their own respective exodus experiences: the Philistines from Caphtor (Crete) and the Arameans from Kir (Mesopotamia).

This equal status emphasis sets the stage for the message of verse 8: "All nations are on equal status with God. All nations are to live responsibly before God. Consequently, all nations who sin—whether Israel, Ethiopia,

Philistia or Syria—will be punished by God. God's judgment is certain."

Verses 9-10 conclude Amos' "certainty-of-judgment" theme and also close out the record of the prophet's ministry. The ever creative Amos used the image of a sieve to drive home his point. A sieve consisted of a large mesh through which grain would be poured in order to separate the chaff from the good grain. The sieve would catch the undesirable debris—the stones, the trash, the waste—and allow the good grain to pass through.

Amos declared that God's judgment on Israel would be like this sifting process. God, the divine sifter, would shake Israel with a "sieve." The outcome would be disasterous; as a result of this divine sifting, "no pebble shall fall upon the earth. All the sinners of my people shall die by the sword" (vv. 9-10). Even those Israelites who never "got" Amos' message—who insisted that being God's chosen people gave them some type of immunity from judgment (v. 10b)—were trapped in the divine sieve and killed by the sword.

Amos' point was candid and blunt. God's judgment was certain. The people of Israel—who "for three transgressions and for four" failed to practice justice and righteousness—were caught in the divine sieve. Not one of them would escape (9:1-4). The nation would come to an end.

Questions for Reflection

1. What were the five visions of Amos? What message did each vision convey?

2. What did Amos mean by the statement, "I am no prophet nor a prophet's son"?

3. How was Amaziah a proponent of institutional religion?

4. Why can Amos be characterized as advocating experiential religion?

Notes

[1]Eugene H. Peterson, *Working the Angles: the Shape of Pastoral Authority* (Grand Rapids MI: Eerdmans, 1987) 1.

[2]James Limburg, *Hosea-Micah*, "Interpretation: A Biblical Commentary for Teaching and Preaching" (Atlanta: John Knox Press, 1988) 116.

[3]The concept of institutional and experiential religion as represented respectively by Amaziah and Amos was introduced to me by Dr. Roy Honeycutt in a classroom lecture at Southern Seminary in Louisville on 24 September 1975.

[4]Limburg, 125.

Epilogue

(Amos 9:11-15)

Verses 11-15 of chapter 9, which speak of the restoration of the Davidic Kingdom and the glorious future age to come, are often regarded as later additions to the original book of Amos. There are several major reasons for holding this view.

(1) The vocabulary does not generally correspond with the vocabulary that Amos used. Specifically, expressions such as "the days of old" (9:11) and "restore the fortunes of my people" (9:14) are characteristic of prophetic literature written after the exile (Isa 63:9; Jer 29:14; Joel 3:18).

(2) The historical setting of these verses is later than the time of Amos. The reference to "the booth of David that is fallen" (9:11), replete with its "ruins" and its "breaches," speaks of a time after Jerusalem (the city of David) had fallen and after the temple had been destroyed. Such a time frame would have been near or during the time of the Babylonian exile (587–538 B.C.), which is much later than the date of 760 B.C. that is attributed to the ministry of Amos.

(3) The utopian-like description of what the future will be like "on that day" (9:11, 13-15) stands in sharp contrast to the gloomy description of the future "day of the Lord" described by Amos (5:18-20). Even more telling perhaps is how this marvelous future is not described. The themes of justice and righteousness that so dominate the message of Amos are not mentioned in 9:13-15. One can scarcely believe that Amos—if he had predicted and

portrayed a future time of restoration and good fortune—
would have done so without a single mention of justice
and righteousness.[1]

Amos 9:11-15, then, is post-Amos in orientation.
This does not mean, however, that this passage serves no
purpose in understanding either Amos or the God whom
he served. Indeed, these verses reflect a future hope that
Amos may very well have possessed:

—a hope that honesty and divine conviction prevented
    Amos from preaching to the stubbornly sinful peo-
    ple of his own generation
—a hope that enabled him to keep on preaching God's
    message of judgment to a people who were already
    doomed
—a hope that, though the Northern Kingdom would cer-
    tainly be destroyed, God could somehow still use
    Amos' prophetic preaching of gloom and doom for
    some type of positive purpose
—a hope that held open the possibility that God could
    somehow (even in ways that from a human per-
    spective seemed contradictorily mysterious) fashion
    a new start from an old ending
—a hope that the God who called Amos from his job as a
    shepherd to go North and preach a message of
    doom could somehow instill a spirit of "possibility"
    into a seemingly impossible situation
—a hope that God, even in the midst of the prophet's
    "preach-judgment-and-destruction" ministry, could
    somehow still have for Amos (and for all future
    generations of God's followers) a word of hope.

Question for Reflection

1. Why is Amos 9:11-15 often viewed as a later addition to the book of Amos?

Note

[1]R. Martin-Achard and S. Paul Re'emi, *Amos and Lamentations: God's People in Crisis*, International Theological Commentary (Edinburgh: The Handsel Press LTD, 1984) 66-67.